THE TAO OF WORK FU

Principles, Practices and Possibilities to Accelerate Your Effectiveness at Work for the Rest of Your Career

STEVE CHAD

The Tao of Work Fu

First published in 2016 by

Panoma Press Ltd
48 St Vincent Drive, St Albans, Herts, AL1 5SJ, UK
info@panomapress.com
www.panomapress.com

Book design and layout by Neil Coe.

Printed on acid-free paper from managed forests.

ISBN 978-1-909623-99-6

The right of Steve Chad to be identified as the author of this work has been asserted in accordance with sections 77 and 78 of the Copyright, Designs and Patents Act 1988.

A CIP catalogue record for this book is available from the British Library.

All rights reserved. No part of this book may be reproduced in any material form (including photocopying or storing in any medium by electronic means and whether or not transiently or incidentally to some other use of this publication) without the written permission of the copyright holder except in accordance with the provisions of the Copyright, Designs and Patents Act 1988. Applications for the copyright holder's written permission to reproduce any part of this publication should be addressed to the publishers.

This book is available online and in bookstores.

Copyright 2015 Steve Chad

For my Mum, Dad and Grandad,
who all fed my hunger to learn.

CONTENTS

Introduction		7
CHAPTER 1	CHANGE	21
CHAPTER 2	COMMUNICATION	61
CHAPTER 3	RELATIONSHIPS	81
CHAPTER 4	MAKING DECISIONS	101
CHAPTER 5	THE ART & SCIENCE OF GETTING THINGS DONE	121
CHAPTER 6	IMAGINATION	145
CHAPTER 7	EFFECTIVE LEARNING	165
CHAPTER 8	THE BEDROCK OF SELLING	193
Acknowledgements		213
About the Author		214
Notes		215

INTRODUCTION

This book, at its core, is written with the intention of helping you to accelerate your effectiveness at work, making you more effective, more quickly, and giving you solid foundational skills and understandings that will continuously serve you for the rest of your career. The title takes inspiration from Chinese philosophy. The words of the well-known phrase Gung Fu (Kung-Fu) translate respectively as Gung: 'work', 'effort' or 'achievement' and Fu: '(hu)man'. Despite its modern association with martial arts, Gung Fu originally refers to any skill that can be achieved through continued human effort and practice. Tao is a word used to describe variously a path, a way or the nature of something. Hence, in borrowing some of these recognisable elements and combining with a little English, we have the Tao of Work Fu, or 'The Way of Human Work'.

It does not attempt to be the definitive text on any specific area of knowledge. Nor by writing it have I attempted to provide a single model upon which the whole world can make sense. What I hope it does is to provide insight into several critical aspects of work that I have found from my own experiences are often overlooked, forgotten about, or in many cases are never learnt at all, but which lay the foundations upon which the rest of the endless mountains of knowledge about work that you may accumulate through the years can be allowed to take firm footing. I hope that it will allow you to develop habits and attitudes towards work that enable you to become more effective at whatever you do to make a living on a regular basis. I hope that it inspires your pursuit of deeper and more detailed understanding of some, if not all of the topics covered. And if you are already well acquainted with some or all of the elements covered, then I hope it can at least provide further confirmation as to their effectiveness when you choose to take action in shaping your career rather than just letting work happen to you.

WHY IS THIS BOOK RELEVANT NOW?

From a personal point of view, I believe that a book like this has always been needed to fill in some of the gaps between separate disciplines with insight into how some of their shared aspects can teach us more about how they can be more effective for us. Incredible advances in technology are enabling productivity like never before, but technology is at heart still merely a tool and unless we understand how and why to use it, its proliferation only provides us with more potential ways of getting things wrong. I felt that my experience to this point in my career was sufficient for me to try and share some of the insights I have gained so that you can find and apply some consistently relevant whys and hows to your own situation and get the most from the opportunities and tools that you have.

Situationally speaking, work is becoming an ever larger part of our lives. There is increasing competition for entry into the workplace and even when you have a job, for other positions that become available. As a result, people are putting ever more time and effort into gaining qualifications that can differentiate them in their fields. But as we shall see, qualifications are not the only reason for people to employ others. In fact more and more emphasis is being placed on being able to find staff who in addition to demonstrating their competence re: understanding the required knowledge about a given field (which is usually currently tested only by observing what qualifications a person has), can also demonstrate the ability to put it to use effectively on a consistent basis in unfamiliar situations that test their abilities to adapt this knowledge, while also involving others in their work (i.e. not solely relying on their own efforts to achieve results).

INTRODUCTION

The infinitesimal number of different outcomes that the massive number of variables in real life bring to the party make applying learning much trickier, and require additional 'meta-skills' to bring the right combination of a person's capabilities together and make them effective at what they do. These meta-skills are usually acquired through time, experience and in some cases simply luck; while this book cannot replace all of those (as we shall see in the chapter on learning, especially not the experience element), by finding and choosing to read it, you will have taken a big step towards being able to:

- Travel through time! Well, you can at least accelerate your progress through several aspects of learning about work simply by becoming more aware of critical issues that are highly valuable for you to know.

- Get lucky! Or for the more practically minded among you, by virtue of your own efforts in doing something to lead you to this point, you will have effectively made your own luck.

This increase in time and effort that we are putting into our jobs is starting to blur the lines between work and personal time, with people working from home, or putting in extra hours in an attempt to keep up with their workload and 'stay ahead'. More and more people are deciding that if they are going to be committing to their careers in such a way, it may as well be in a field that particularly appeals to them – making the distinction between the two even fuzzier. The increasing number of entrepreneurs choosing to plough their own furrow know that running your own business can take up more personal time than they could ever have imagined. And the growing numbers of career coaches and encouragement of entrepreneurialism from banks, governments and other business institutions is only encouraging this movement. The ability to choose a career, shape it according to your preferred direction, and follow your true calling is rapidly becoming more accessible than ever; likewise technology is giving us the ability to be able to work at any time, night or day, in virtually any place that a satellite signal or at least power can reach and, even then, for periods in places where it can't. Therefore, being able to differentiate and shine in terms of the value we offer as individuals is important. Much of your success and future opportunity may rest upon your reputation – even if this is only within your own office – and being able to build a solid one (reputation) requires sustainable, repeated activity. It doesn't happen with a single quick fix, but requires time and effort, plus the knowledge of how and where to apply them.

GETTING THE FOUNDATIONS RIGHT

Through having worked with a wide variety of people in both team and individual situations, from inductions to providing crash courses in new technologies and methodologies, I have realised that getting the essentials right is of vital importance. In some instances, this required me to strip down often lengthy and complex subjects into the core lessons that people could pick up in the space of a couple of hours, or sometimes even minutes. This is one of the core reasons for this book – enabling people who are new to the workplace, and even those who are not so new, to grasp quickly the essentials of working effectively, and eventually make them second nature.

By exploring these core elements, I hope to be able to help reduce your fear of things like steep learning curves – enabling you to progress along them more quickly and also reduce some of the pain associated with them. That's not to say there will not be any pain or discomfort; as we will see later in the book, this is a natural part of any learning process but by providing you with some understanding, I hope that these elements of the process can be minimised in duration – and, bearing in mind what we will find out about perception, made less painful as you will be equipped with the knowledge that things can and usually do get better, rather than staying trapped in a never-ending loop of failure, worry and self-directed remorse. I also want to help you develop the ways in which you think. To foster the possibilities available to you by getting you more readily used to asking of situations, of yourself and of others: 'What if?'

Parts of the book are designed to provide you with some practical frameworks and structures that help you to organise your thoughts and actions – making your daily work easier to manage so that you can spend more time focusing on high-value activities such as those which create and develop breakthroughs and insights, while both simplifying the low-value, simple, repetitive ones such as firefighting (dealing with problems) and removing time wasted worrying about how to manage the work required; basically, helping you to achieve more and procrastinate less.

Closely related to this is the skill of getting you into the habit of executing, by removing the typical barriers that hold us back. This is often a case of simply looking at the next thing we need to or can do and doing that, rather than being paralysed by the overawing sight of the whole task every time we attempt to make any progress.

Holistic Self-Sustainability

The types of skills and knowledge that I hope to share with you are based upon an approach similar to that espoused by the field of Organisational Development (OD). Instead of just prescribing a fix for a given situation, my intent is to provide you with knowledge that you will find can be useful throughout your working life, knowledge that provides you with value beyond the initial learning curve of getting accustomed to the way in which 'work works', so to speak. In the OD world, consultancy advice is provided with a view to helping the client be able to develop continuously and sustain themselves once the agreed scope of consultancy work is complete. To put it in a way with which we are all probably a lot more familiar, we could use the maxim, "Give a man a fish and he feeds himself for a day. Teach him to fish and he can feed himself for life."

In terms of how I will attempt to do that, I have tried to avoid giving out only 'fish' – stand-alone pieces of knowledge – and instead have focused on providing flexible, versatile and transferrable knowledge in the form of:

- Principles – these are lessons or rules that have stood the test of time. Occasionally you may encounter a scenario where it may prove expedient to ignore the principle. I hope that my explanation of why they are important is of help in your decision, so that at least you will acknowledge and understand why sometimes making an exception may be OK in the short term, but if exceptions are made on a consistent, long-term basis, (i.e. consistent ignorance of the principle) it is likely to lead to disaster. They are, in essence, guidelines to help direct you, and you will find that they aid more often than not.

- Practical Skills & Methodologies – as the old English saying goes, "There's more than one way to skin a cat." In work, there are also a great many different ways, models and methods that you can use to achieve any given objective. While I have gone into some detail explaining the importance and function of some of those methodologies I have shared with you, they are not the only methods available and I encourage you to explore them and other models more deeply in order to get a really good understanding of their strengths, weaknesses and relevancies to the situations you will face. Essentially, I have attempted to provide you with a model or method that is effective and easy to understand, pick up and use straight away and summarised the key steps that you would typically need to get you started on using it – which is one of the crucial steps towards learning and better understanding it in a real world practical context!

- A Possibilities Mindset – in some parts of the book, I have attempted to open your mind to the fact that the world is so full of unexplored knowledge, concepts and ideas and that it can really pay off to at least consider, explore and evaluate some new ones from time to time as opposed to holding a mindset that is unaware of such possibilities, or closed to accepting anything beyond what you already know or are comfortable with. In short, whether it comes to you from an outside source, springs from the creativity of your own mind or is generated by a stimulation of one by the other, everything that you could possibly need to know or understand is already out there (or in there) somewhere; all you need to do is recognise it to be able to start exploring and making use of it.

AVOIDING THE EXTREMISM TRAP

In expanding the possibilities and variety of tools and options that an open mind makes available to you, I am also encouraging you to try out new methods and approaches so that you don't get trapped by 'extremism'. By extremism, I'm not necessarily talking about religious or political extremism, but simply about the principle of doing the same thing in the same way to the exclusion of all else, whether it's because you believe it is the only way, or always the best way or perhaps simply because you have never stopped to consider that there may be other ways.

Bruce Lee, the famous martial artist respected for his views on continual development and refinement of what is effective in his field once said, "Nothing can survive long by going to extremes." This applies to practically everything we look at, be it physical or metaphysical (i.e. a thought or concept). While it can be useful to push the limits occasionally, staying in that extreme place or state is a recipe for becoming blinkered, rigid and obsolete. As we shall see in the chapter on change, if we stand still, events and the rest of the world will keep moving and overtake us.

Utilising only one tool, methodology or mindset severely limits our ability to change and adapt to the changes around us. To use a metaphor, if you are only using a hammer, suddenly everything looks like a nail – and some things don't take too well to being hit. But similarly, trying to utilise all of your tools all the time is equally an extreme. At work, this is typified by the person who insists on following every single step of a process or manual, whether it is relevant or not – following a proscribed process for its own sake. Not every one of them is necessary all the time. Knowing what is necessary and what isn't comes with experience, and that's the purpose of this book – sharing some of mine with you in order to speed up your learning to some degree.

In essence, I am saying that being aware of multiple options and elements is useful, but experience will show you that being able to discern what works in a given situation and what doesn't will help you to get better at utilising the right tool for the job. As with Bruce Lee's approach to martial arts, he described Jeet Kune Do, his later approach to fighting, as not being a style, but just such a philosophy where whatever tool was right for the situation should be used, anything else stripped away.[1] Not fixating on one style or set of arbitrary techniques alone, but being aware of the core dynamics of the situation and applying something that is both relevant and effective, regardless of its origin. I would describe this approach as 'contextualism': being prepared to use what fits.

WORK AS A JOURNEY

To fully understand why I have adopted this approach, I believe it will help to explain the context of where both the book and my own outlook on work are coming from. I believe work, like life itself, is a journey. We may enter the world of work with an objective of where we want it to take us; alternatively we may only have general ideas of what we want to attain from it, and sometimes we may not know or give time to thinking about where we want to go.

I have experienced many of these mindsets, and continue to move between them depending on various influences and cycles of drive and consolidation that I go through, but one thing I have learnt about myself here is that each destination I set is not my ultimate goal.

For starters, what happens if and when I reach it? While my accomplishments may not be considered to be on the same scale as Olympic gold medal winning athletes, they are nevertheless my goals, leading me to potentially be confronted by the same conundrum: once completed, what now?

Chances are, we'll go looking for the next one, and if we can find a good enough reason, we will invest a lot of our time and effort into achieving it. It may be a short-term goal. It may be a purely selfish one. It may be that we embark upon a new almighty quest to effect a very big change, perhaps the type that we know cannot be fully realised in our lifetime, but for which we will have laid the foundations for others to continue and attain the goal. Either way, there will always be something else for us to follow, build or seek, and however intensely we pursue it, having a set of tools and skills that allow us to do so effectively while gradually developing our own capabilities along the way will help us to enjoy and gain more satisfaction from the journey whatever our current and future goals are.

Whether it happens on an ad hoc basis or as the result of a long-term plan, flow theory suggests that being able to feel as though we are making continuous progress can have a beneficial effect on our well-being.

ENJOY THE RIDE

In addition to what your goals are, how you reach your destination will also become important, as this will have an effect on your level of happiness throughout your career. As already mentioned, work/life boundaries are blurring and more people are electing to make work an even bigger part of their lives through self-employment, but even for a standard 9-to-5 worker, work will take up a hugely significant piece of your life. Around half of your waking hours on most weekdays will be spent at work, and many of us will spend much of the remainder of our free time thinking about it.

So, if possible, why shouldn't we try to make the journey itself as enjoyable and rewarding as we can in order to live happier and more fulfilling lives? Being able to reflect on personal progress in itself tends to be more conducive to further personal growth, creating a virtuous circle that has been made apparent from the findings of various researchers including Professor Mihaly Csikszentmihalyi. For decades he has been conducting research into a state he calls 'Flow'.[2] Flow is a state of mind wherein a person is completely immersed in a particular activity giving them a sense of energised focus and enjoyment. His research has revealed that the opportunity to experience this feeling or state on a regular basis not only promotes personal development and growth but also increases feelings of competence, efficacy, happiness and satisfaction with life.

In equipping you with such versatile 'meta' tools, I want to help you to continually discover better practices, recognise and be prepared to accept opportunities that come your way, and in turn have the opportunity to appreciate the progress you have made, enriching your journey.

You will notice that I use the phrase 'better' practice quite deliberately instead of 'best' practice, for a number of reasons which I hope reinforce the type of mindset that promotes development. 'Best practice' is in my opinion, quite a claim – who says it's the best practice? How do we know it's the best? Does somebody give out gold medals for it? If it's the best, then presumably we don't need to look any further, and we won't be able to get any better. To me, best practice suggests a closed mindset which has accepted that a pinnacle has been reached, and that no more progress is needed or possible. I prefer to say 'better practice' or simply 'good practice', as this is not as much of an absolute (or if you like, extreme), and helps you to maintain an open-minded point of view that supports the possibility of future improvements.

THE IMPACT OF REALITY UPON THEORY

Countless people have commented on the effect that reality has upon the plans that we make. From the line in Robert Burns' apologetic poem *To a Mouse* whose nest he had just overturned with his plough, "The best laid schemes o' mice an' men, Gang aft agley,"[3] (translation into modern-day English, "The best laid plans of mice and men often go awry"), to the military maxim, "No plan survives first contact with the enemy," the principle that connects the two is clear: life and the real world contain such an infinite number of variables which can come into play at any point in time that it is impossible for anyone to execute everything perfectly according to the original plan all the time.

Some parts of the plan may go as expected, and the smaller scale or simpler the plan, the higher the chance of this happening; for instance, scientifically controlled laboratory experiments, where specific activities are tested for specific outcomes in tightly controlled environments where attempts to remove all variables except the one being tested are removed.

But take those experiments out of the lab, and expose them to the gazillion influences in motion at any one time in the world at large, and predictability of outcome suddenly becomes much less certain. This is, in essence, what chaos theory is all about – the fact that the tiniest change in one part of the world (or even universe) could be the trigger for a chain of events which lead to much more significant changes further on, and that there are so many possible outcomes to any one expected event that absolutely anything is possible within or even beyond the realms of our imagination.

The bottom line of all this incalculable prevarication about possibilities and variations is that planning and structure can help up to a point, but awareness of dynamics and some degree of agility will also be essential to cope with the unforeseen circumstances that the world can and will throw up. And as we accept that we cannot accurately predict the future (the first person to create a crystal ball will become very, very rich and sought after) so we should recognise that there is no single, perfect path through life. Outside influences will affect what we need to adapt to, and will also influence our own thoughts and direction, and indeed our own goals may change over time. Even if you choose a highly specialised career path, the chances are that even within that field you will need to be flexible and versatile enough to deal with a certain amount of variety that could come your way. The best we can do is equip ourselves with a set of tools, skills and outlooks that improve our chances of being able to adapt to, take advantage of and enjoy the benefits of whatever opportunities our work life throws up.

HUMAN POTENTIAL

As you may be beginning to pick up from the style of my writing, I believe that as humans we each have massive potential. Nothing makes me happier than being able to help people realise it and release it. At this point, I believe I have both the right intent and sufficient capability to be able to do so to some degree. Thus, I decided to help people begin at the beginning, by focusing on building a highly versatile set of core essential skills with lifetime value. Sound, progressive foundations that can be applied throughout your career.

That's not to say that you couldn't get a lot from the book if you aren't new to the workplace. You will doubtless encounter many of the principles and approaches in this book throughout your work life in different forms, sometimes in more detail or seen from new points of view. You may have encountered or even already used and studied in depth some of the models and methodologies herein. If this is you, I still believe that there is plenty of value for you to find here – whether it be refreshment or realisation of some of the principles at play in your daily activities, or encountering new ideas and perspectives that may not have occurred to you before. As I have said throughout, this book is a starting point for a great many pathways, not a definitive stopping-point, so whether you use the content as is, or it stimulates or excites you to explore some of the topics further, then hopefully either of these outcomes means that I have achieved my objective.

You may notice that I repeat certain themes over and over throughout the book. This is in part simply the consequence of taking a holistic view, where some themes continuously interweave and either reappear or have an influence in many different areas. But it is a deliberate style on my part, as later, when we see the effect that repetition (and the lack of it) has upon learning, you will understand why I have chosen to take numerous opportunities to remind you of and reinforce what I regard as some of the more critical topics in the book.

In each chapter, I will attempt to demonstrate why the topic is of particular importance at work, explain the dynamics of some of its fundamental principles, and in most cases provide a simple practical method to help you feel confident enough to start utilising it. This single first step (taking action to try something new and find out that the consequences are nowhere near as scary as we think) is the most important one that will see you progress quickly along the learning curve and even decide to explore some new directions, and learn in the process.

DIFFERENT WAYS TO USE THIS BOOK

If I give you a single, definitive description of how to use this book, I might be limiting its potential (for starters, it probably makes a great decoration for your shelves, a moderately effective coffee/tea/beer mat, or a barely ergonomic paperweight!). Drawing on some of the ideas you will encounter in the chapter on imagination, specifically those relating to utilisation, I would suggest the following as possible ways that could prove effective, but leave the potential methods of what works for you up to you and your situation/ inspiration/ mood.

Use The Method That Works For You

You could read it all through at once – this will have the effect of pulling a lot of the concepts together and making a little more sense as many of the subjects overlap and make reference to one another.

You could read it and then summarise the key elements from each chapter into bullets. I often find this is quite a good way of remembering many

INTRODUCTION

of the points that I find particularly relevant or useful, as it requires me to repeat it, understand it sufficiently to be able to produce my own synthesised version, and provides the stimulus of creativity that gives me more of a sense of accomplishment. Please don't let the fact that I have done this for you at the end of each chapter deter you from creating a more concise and entertaining version of your own with which to wow friends, colleagues, and potential life partners at your depth and variety of topical conversation points.

You could keep it handy as a work life reference tool – to dip in and out of on particular subjects when you encounter different scenarios (conducting the bullet activity really helps you cut to the chase in this respect).

Ideally after reading all the way through, rather than try to remember it all (you probably won't) or run screaming/hide away from the mountain of knowledge and information that you now feel you need to understand to be successful (you probably will), I would suggest you try applying one element at a time – try it, get used to doing it, and then when you think it's becoming a habit, try another one. This is the step-by-step approach to breaking down and achieving large and complex tasks that you will encounter later. It is one of the themes that appear continually throughout the book because it works and is incredibly flexible in terms of its utility; you will see then why I recommend this method.

Discuss elements of the book with friends and colleagues – use it as a starting point for further learning. By debating, stretching and testing the concepts and principles, you will get better at understanding their dynamics, what their limitations might be, and when might be a good time to utilise them. It will also help you to identify new areas that you feel you need to understand, so that you can take your learning and development beyond the points made in the book – self-driven evolution!

But if I were to suggest how you could really get the most from the book, I would suggest doing all of these. The different types of learning you can experience from reading and acting upon the content of this book will be of value throughout your working life, so the more deeply you can understand and embed them as part of your natural approach to work, the better.

I thank you for taking the time to listen to my thoughts and sincerely wish that this book gives you as much hope and inspiration in the reading as it gave me writing it.

CHAPTER 1
CHANGE

So, first things first, why a chapter on change? And is there any particular reason why it's the first one up? To answer both of these questions at the same time, the fact that change happens is one of the most pervasive and yet fundamental principles of the universe in which we live, and understanding that is vital to gaining greater insight into any of the other things this book will attempt to help you with, or to any of the things that you will attempt in the future, whether that be on your own, or with other people.

Let's establish one thing: change is inevitable. It's coming from everywhere, all the time, it's going out to everywhere all the time, it's happening everywhere, all the time. The second law of thermodynamics states that everything in the universe is in a constant state of growing entropy – i.e. everything is constantly moving from a state of stability and order to one of increased disorder and randomness. It sounds a bit scary, right? If the universe is against us, what's the point of trying? Well, of course, many of these universal changes are happening so gradually or on a level so far beyond our normal scope of observation that we can't even notice them (such as evolutionary changes on earth, the ongoing depletion of the sun's power, or the molecular breakdown of chemical reactions), but the point is that everything in the entire universe is constantly changing, and by their very nature, these changes are having an effect on other things around them.

Every single action of every single waking minute of every day that any of us take is influenced by changes we experience, and in turn, itself, will cause further change. When we are sleeping, we are doing things to our environment: using oxygen and resources. Even when we're not doing much at all, but just being here, we are influencing other parts of the world by our very presence: we are consuming something – food, oxygen – and influencing other things – by communication, or simply by the impact of our weight upon the thing on which we are standing, sitting or lying. Just by thinking we are creating possibilities and potential influences that could drive us, or others, in particular directions.

Even the things that aren't living or moving are influencing what happens next in the world simply by their presence; wet weather outside isn't exactly a living entity, but it is dynamic and causes me to put on my wellingtons – and if I don't have any, it may cause me to go shopping for some. And the road crossing that has been painted at some point in the past may cause me to slow down in case there are people walking across the road.

So it is an understatement to say that there are trillions upon trillions of causes and effects combining and recombining at any one time, and continuously throughout time, each of which will have some kind of impact on our world. Just for a moment try to imagine how much change that means! (But not for too long, I don't want you to drift away into the infinities of mind space forever.)

This is the foundation of chaos theory. Sometimes called the Butterfly Effect after a presentation by Professor of Meteorology Edward N. Lorenz to the American Association for the Advancement of Science in 1972,[4] it dictates that with such an almost infinite number of changes happening at every level (from huge, globally catastrophic geological events down to those occurring at a microscopic and sub-atomic level), with the sheer volume of potential outcomes from the even more unfathomable number of combinations of any of these changes acting together, given enough time, anything is possible.

The term Butterfly Effect simply describes a possible example of the result of such a combination: a theoretical butterfly flaps its wings setting in motion a chain of events; the wing flap causes a slight change in air pressure near another insect, which causes it to take evasive action from what it thinks may be a predator. It runs into a dark space which turns out to be a sensitive mechanism, which causes a malfunction in the machine, which results in an emergency situation and leads to a nuclear meltdown.

OK, this is an extreme view of quite an enormous topic. If we spent all day trying to get our heads around the full potential consequences of our every action we wouldn't ever do anything else, it would be a pointless and endless task, and nobody has a crystal ball. The main takeaway from this section is to understand that no matter what we do, or how we try to avoid it, change is all around us, all the time, and in fact we are a part of it, so to constantly attempt to avoid one of the fundamental forces of our universe is likely to end in failure – however hard we try and fight it, *some* change will occur.

WE NEED CHANGE – AND ACTUALLY WE'RE QUITE GOOD AT IT

OK, so we've figured out that we're living in the midst of a swirling morass of constant change that could lead to anything happening at any time, from an annoying itch to the sinking of the *Titanic*. It's not all bad news though. Every single thing in the universe has had to undergo constant change to get to its current state, including us. Our very own evolution is a story of change, it's how we got here to the point where we are now able to enjoy and appreciate whatever luxuries come our way.

Of course, change may not always be viewed as good. Note that I say 'viewed as'. I use these exact words because our definition of what is good or bad is in fact based upon individual perceptions. We each have a completely different map of the world. As the saying goes, "One man's meat is another man's poison." The same things can have very different meanings and consequences for each of us; the labels 'good' and 'bad' are simply perceptions and as such are open to being changed themselves.

As we know, our own tastes and opinions – a type of perception – can change greatly over time or even from one moment to the next. I usually take two spoons of sugar in a cup of coffee, but if I drink it while eating milk chocolate, the relative effect of the very sweet chocolate makes the coffee taste (to me) like it has no sugar in it. But it is still the same two-sugar coffee, and would taste that sweet to most other people unless they had also succumbed to a choc-fest or were three-spoons freaks.

Any definitions we have are simply personal ones at that point in time. If we take a look at some of the elements of society which consistently appear to be slow to change, such as laws and even dictionaries, we find they are simply moving according to currently agreed perceptions; examples of how humans have recognised the need to try and find common ground between our own unique points of view in order to be able to work together, as that is generally held as one of the most effective ways for us to survive and progress. Laws are updated to reflect changes in society, and new words are added to dictionaries usually after being generated and embraced by large chunks of society itself.

If we have a natural inclination to want to change even the most stuffy and rooted things – for both logical reasons, and because we have an innate drive to try and advance ourselves – then why does change have such a reputation for making us so uncomfortable that a whole field has evolved (Change Management) just to work out how best to implement and deal with it in the workplace? Why, despite being surrounded by so much change all day, every day, do we believe that we are generally averse to it, and often bad at it?

We take thousands of complex decisions and actions every day as we make our way through this constantly changing world and deal quite comfortably with their consequences, so logically it could therefore be said that we are actually quite good at change management. The number of bad experiences is dwarfed by the number of experiences that work out fine (we could nominally classify any experience that helps us, boosts our mood or at least doesn't damage us, as a good one), but for some reason, we often choose to dwell on the relatively small number of negative experiences and let them influence our actions more intensely.

So we must ask the question, why do these negative experiences have so much more of an impact upon our future thinking than the far greater number of positive or at least non-negative ones?

Confirmation bias may have something to do with part of the answer. This describes the human brain's tendency to search for, interpret or recall information in a way that confirms our existing beliefs. Intensely painful or emotionally uncomfortable experiences are usually remembered a lot more easily than the myriad of moderately pleasant ones which we probably experience on a much more regular basis, so naturally are likely to be more prominent and poignant in our thinking when we try to reference any previous experiences we may have had which are similar to a new situation. But why is this so? The answer to why negative emotion is more memorable is all to do with the way our mind is wired.

HOW THE WAY WE THINK AFFECTS CHANGE

Change in itself isn't necessarily good or bad and it would be foolishly simplistic to classify all change as being exclusively so one way or the other. It simply acquires such labels due to our individual opinions of whether it is good for us. While this makes our reaction to change a highly individualised matter of personal opinion, one of the most consistent factors that can influence our perception and make us all feel uncomfortable with change is the unknown aspect of it.

Most of those changes that we deal with without thinking or fear are familiar to us – we understand a lot about the context of the situation, and the likely dynamics and consequences of the change. Often they are so familiar to us that handling them has become habit and is done without thinking about it or even noticing that we have done so. But when we encounter situations with what we regard as a significant amount of unknown information, we typically become less comfortable about what could happen. In many cases, left alone, our minds will dream up the worst case scenario making us anxious, uptight and less effective at working and cooperating with others and the reason for this lies in how our brains have developed through history.

Way back in the earlier days of our evolution, the environment in which we were living was very different; there were more wild animals randomly on the loose and no civilised society as we understand it today. Our primitive brains therefore had to evolve to help us survive in this environment which meant they became good at two core things: being able to recognise rewards in order to take advantage of them and prolong our survival, and being able to recognise threats in order to either avoid or escape them. The main difference between the effects each of these critical factors had upon our thinking lay in impact and timing. If we missed a reward, unless we were already at our last ebb of physical health, it was possible that we would be able to survive until another one came along, and there was a fair chance that we may be able to survive a string of several lost opportunities in a row.

Threats, however, could come in the form of wild animals (or even other humans) that may have wanted to eat or attack us. The odds of survival from failing to recognise even one such instance would have been a lot lower than those stemming from missing an opportunity.

As it happens, parts of our brain evolved to become quite good at noticing change – whether that is the rustling of undergrowth, or a small change in someone's appearance that we can't quite put our finger on, but somehow we feel as though we can almost instinctively sense that something is different. And in evolving to deal with detected change, evolution placed more emphasis on being able to recognise threats than rewards (due to the greater impact of failing to detect them) and gave them priority in our thought processes.

Decision making on this level happens largely in a part of our brain called the limbic system (often referred to as the 'lizard brain'). It sees things in black and white terms with no middle ground. Is this thing I detect good or bad? (Reward or threat.) And because of the potential impact of a threat, it defaults to regarding every new thing as just that unless it finds evidence to the contrary. What happens when a change is evaluated negatively? Back in our distant past, there were three main instinctive reactions: fight, flight or freeze (hope that we hadn't been seen and the danger would either lose interest or not regard us as something it needed to attack or eat).

Now this was effective back in the days when we were having to deal regularly with the possibility of wild animals wanting to eat or maim us, but such extreme reactions are not so good in modern society. To maintain a sustainable society we need to have objective reactions to new situations so that discussion and objective action can be taken, not animalistic ones, which tend to be more extreme and can isolate individuals and destroy civilised group dynamics.

Our lizard brain is easily roused by perceived threats, and being the safety system that protects us from the largest of them (i.e. to our very survival), it has priority until it feels it is safe for the slower, objective part to take over. It is also extremely difficult to overcome by sheer force of will. Dr. Steve Peters, former psychiatrist to the all-conquering GB Cycling team, describes it as being like a chimpanzee, much stronger than the rational 'human' side of our personalities.[5] But it can be managed so that it doesn't feel threatened by the situation.

To do that on a consistent basis, we have to avoid falling into the trap of acting purely on the basis of emotional reaction. We may still have strong emotions about something, but in understanding what is happening to us we are better placed to take steps to prevent them controlling our immediate reactions and allowing our conscious brains to make more reasoned decisions. Managing our emotions in this way is called emotional regulation.

Emotional Regulation

Having the ability to regulate oneself emotionally is now generally regarded as a key skill for anyone wishing to go into management, but I would go a step further. Being able to deal objectively with change and the unknown is one of the keys to achieving any degree of sustained workplace success for anyone. Without this ability we simply cease to be able to function effectively, whether that be alongside others or simply even on our own. Let's take a look at some ways in which we can reduce our brain's propensity to view things with suspicion simply because we have an information gap.

Recognition & Labelling

The practice of labelling (i.e. giving a name to something) is a form of stated recognition. As we saw in the threat/reward evaluation that our brains constantly play out, by not knowing about something we have a knowledge gap which makes us uncomfortable – we begin to adopt an adverse reaction towards whatever is the focus of our concern. By giving a name, or label, to the unknown element, be it an object, situation or feeling, we are then able to associate it with the things we know about the label we gave. In effect, we are defining its characteristics by association with something else and filling in many of the knowledge gaps, making it less scary. It has become more familiar to us, and by referencing our understanding of the label words, we can begin to believe that we are gaining some control over the situation or our feelings. We can reference and model how we have dealt with the recognised object/situation/feeling before, giving us more of a sense of control and making it more likely that we avoid the fight/flight/freeze state of mind which makes analytical thought difficult. We then have more chance of viewing the focus of our attention objectively or to good effect. Enabling reference to recognised sets of information about these areas allows us to believe we are able to influence the situation and assert some degree of control over both it and our own destiny. This reduces that anxiety of the lizard brain, opening the door for reasoned evaluation.

Here's an example: your manager asks you for a meeting first thing on Monday. You may get a little anxious at what this meeting could be about. Left to its own devices, your lizard brain might begin to get defensive about the worst possible scenario so it can prepare sufficient defensive tactics. Has there been a complaint about my work? Have I made a big mistake? Am I not delivering to expectations?

By the simple act of recognising that this could possibly be the result of our brain's self-defence mechanism getting carried away with itself, we can at least notice that there may be an issue with the way we are thinking this through, and have a chance of taking some action to remedy the situation, calm ourselves down or relieve the worry we are imagining. We may be able to dismiss it as silly negative thought and only perception – but even if we can't do that, just recognising that our current feelings are the result of a known process can provide enough light at the end of the tunnel to limit any further escalation of the anxiety we have built up to this point.

So the next time you feel your anxiety levels increasing, try acknowledging to yourself that it's just your brain's way of trying to protect you. You are labelling the situation and buying yourself some time (and calm) to figure out a good course of action that will help, by recognising your feelings and understanding that you don't necessarily have to head down a tunnel that sees you randomly veer out of control, but that you are undergoing a natural process that can be managed, and you have options.

Reappraisal

Sometimes, however, our feelings of discomfort are stronger, and we need a more powerful method of calming our natural reactions. Reappraisal is such a method, and can help us to avoid the descent into anxiety simply by taking a different view of the situation.

As we know, our view of the world is based simply upon our perception of it. A singular view. There are countless other ways of looking at any situation we find ourselves in. If we see a video of soldiers getting blown up, we may be horrified. If we recognise the soldiers, we may be sad. Some people may be impressed at the spectacle of the explosion itself. If we are told that it is a fictional film, our viewpoint may change. We may also become impressed at the spectacle. Depending on the type of film, or who we believe the soldiers to be, we may even be satisfied or pleased that the 'bad guys' have got their just deserts, and might even cheer. If we find out that the consequence of this action causes a different outcome other than that of fictional bad guys getting their just deserts, we may feel sad about it again. So here we have seen how many different views can grow out of the same situation, changing under the influence of different information.

This is what reappraisal attempts to help us do. By keeping an open mind, and looking at something from a different perspective, we can get a better feeling of whether our emotional reaction really is the correct one. (Here's a clue, most of the time it probably isn't, especially in the workplace.) In understanding this, again, we give ourselves the time and clarity of thought to be able to take a more reasoned approach to whatever challenges we face.

There are many ways of reappraising situations, but here are a few that work for me:

Multiple Perspectives:

Imagining the situation from somebody else's point of view. You may begin to see several reasons why a person might be acting like they do, or at least recognise that even if you do not know why, you realise that you need to understand more before making a hard judgment. By turning things around, a particular situation may look bad in one sense, but it could also be seen as an opportunity to learn something new, or an excuse to make a change that has been long overdue.

Distance:

Imagine you are looking at the situation from a distance – zooming out and seeing it in the context of a bigger picture, and the implications of different courses of action in terms of that bigger picture. Is it really as big a deal as it seems?

Different Point in Time:

A bit like changing the distance at which you view something, being able to imagine looking back in time at it can really help to shape how important or how big a deal it really is and how you may want to react to it.

Humour:

Often, this is a very quick and, given practice, easy method of dealing with discomfort. Humour can belittle feelings of worry or foreboding and relaxes you, bringing about a more positive and objective state of mind.

Be aware that reappraisal has its potential downside – it is possible for us to 'reappraise down', i.e. imagine a worse situation than we currently believe it to be. Being aware of this and using the zooming out method above can help you avoid getting dragged down this blinkered no-option path.

Practice, as with just about anything, can help you to improve both your effectiveness at using these techniques and your experience of knowing when to use them, and herein lies the key to increasing their effect further: timing. Being able to implement them as early as you can will increase their efficacy in helping you to regulate your emotions. Once emotional anxiety levels reach a certain point, it can be extremely difficult to hold back 'the chimpanzee' and the knee-jerk reactions that it usually displays; but with practice, recognition of when stimulation levels are on the rise allows you to deploy these techniques while there is still a good chance that your mind is willing to listen to them.

If we take a look at what reappraisal is doing, it is in fact helping us to use our brain's natural tendencies to help regulate our emotions. As we have seen earlier, when we are emotionally aroused by what we perceive as a threat, we begin to try and fill in the gaps in our understanding by creating stories in order to give us a sense of control, and a base from which to make 'potentially life-saving' decisions. To keep us safe, these tend to be worst case scenarios, so we accelerate our fight/flight/freeze reactions as a response.

By recognising the early feelings of our defensive reaction and reappraising the situation (upwards), we are in effect creating new stories to fill in the gaps in our understanding. By realising that there are several alternative versions of the story which could be correct (i.e. multiple perceptions of the same thing), we are able to acknowledge that this situation is not definitely a danger to us, calming our emotional reaction, and allowing us to focus on a more objective next step – whether that be taking action to deal with the situation, or to find out more before we act too rashly.

Sleep!

One of the critical tenets of being able to operate effectively (especially when it comes to emotional regulation) is sleep. Having enough sleep can change your whole outlook on life.

The grumpiness that we can exhibit when we don't get enough sleep is just an indicator of a much bigger problem, one that can severely affect how effectively we operate.

The part of our brain that we use for conscious thought processes such as decision making or prioritising (the prefrontal cortex) is often referred to in psychology as the 'goldilocks' part of the brain, as like the character, it needs conditions to be just right for effective operation. Not too much emotional stimulation, not too much overuse. Unfortunately, as this part has only developed relatively recently in our evolutionary history, it has not had time to refine its operational efficiency as well as other parts like the limbic system and as a result it gets very tired very quickly.

To understand how difficult a task the prefrontal cortex has on its hands, envisage David Rock's analogy in *Your Brain At Work*.[6] Imagine that the prefrontal cortex is a stage, and any thoughts, memories or pieces of information you need in order to figure something out are actors helping you to play out the story of whatever you are thinking about. Getting actors on to the stage takes effort. The longer it is since they were utilised, the further away in the audience they are and the more effort it takes to get them on to the stage. Add to this the effort required to organise and utilise the thoughts. Then the effort it takes to get them off the stage when they are not in use. Given that he describes the stage as being so tiny it can only hold a maximum of about three thoughts at any one time and you begin to understand the incredible amount of effort your prefrontal cortex must spend manipulating and jockeying the different thoughts required on to and off the stage as you wrestle with your mental challenge. Put simply, effective conscious thinking is a delicate and difficult activity. Our prefrontal cortex has a lot of mental labour to do in terms of finding, organising and then exploring the often complex and nuanced relationships between many pieces of information while only being able to do so a few pieces at a time. If we are already tired, it becomes so much more difficult and in some cases impossible to focus on the task at hand.

If we look at prioritising, a highly intensive thought process, when we are unable to prioritise clearly we often feel swamped by the enormity of all the tasks and decisions upon us. This is in effect imprisoning us in the 'fear zone' – setting our fight or flight reactions buzzing at the scale of the task we face as we cannot find an answer to the challenge in front of us. Despite it only being a thought, one perception, in the absence of any other cues to remind or prompt us, then it's quite possible that our choice of reaction to the threat of the unknown turns easily to flight – or in work-related terms, task avoidance and procrastination.

Therefore, getting the right amount of sleep can have an amazing effect on both your capacity to think clearly and make well-evaluated decisions, and also on your motivation and, in turn, your whole mood and outlook on the day. Tiredness can make it extremely difficult to focus on anything or to make an objective choice as to what to focus on, and out of the many thoughts that flow through our minds, as we have seen for 'safety first' reasons, we are by default prone to dwell on worst case scenarios. Work life could be viewed as simply a continuous series of progressions – a series of decisions that come one after the other, that can affect one another, and when collected together can have a cumulative effect. So being in a productive, emotionally balanced frame of mind for as much of it as we can is probably a good thing.

While we can often continue to operate for a day or two despite missing a few hours' sleep here and there without seeming to notice it, we are accumulating what is referred to as a 'sleep debt'. Unless your debt is cleared with a good amount of good quality sleep, your decision-making capabilities, performance levels and general mood will nosedive, and matters that you might normally accept and deal with easily can become major obstacles, each one causing you more anxiety and worry – which, as you are tired, you will struggle to rationalise and escape from. How much sleep we each need varies, but take some time to notice what works for you in terms of optimum amount, the best times at which you choose to sleep and what things you do before sleeping (or trying to), and you can go a long way towards avoiding the heavy psychological burden that constant sleep debt brings.

As we shall see in the chapter on learning, getting more practice at something can help us improve our performance at it. However, it is not just about quantity; the more effective our practice is, the better we learn – and if our minds are not in a fit state to make decisions and learn from them, then something has to give and much of the new information we take in will be discarded and lost. This may carry the added danger of making us feel that we are not making any progress and lead to demotivation and other negative, unproductive thought cycles. Getting enough sleep is an extremely simple, yet frequently overlooked way of boosting your capabilities and increasing your happiness and enjoyment levels across the spectrum of your daily work and life experiences.

PROGRESS – LIKE CHANGE, IS A BUMPY RIDE

One thing to remember throughout your encounters with change, whether you are being subjected to it or are trying to implement it, is that there will be good times where you make excellent progress, and there will be times that are not so good – where progress feels wrong, painfully slow or like it isn't happening at all. Change isn't always a linear process, and you may find yourself having to deal with great obstacles or difficulties such as loss of motivation, in yourself or others.

There is an interesting pattern related to the ebb and flow of human reaction to change, which stems from the work of psychologist Elizabeth Kübler-Ross. She was originally studying the effect that death of a family member has on the mental outlook of surviving relatives, and how they deal with its effects in terms of grieving and returning to normal (pre-occurrence) levels of operation in their daily life. She concluded that there is a noticeable process through which many people progress in their journey of learning to live with the loss and it was christened the Kübler-Ross Curve after her work.[7] Some people experience different stages at different times and move through them in different orders, but the generally accepted model expects the following stages to occur:

Shock – the individual expresses surprise at the event often due to lack of full knowledge about it and its sudden impact.

Denial – the individual refuses to believe that the event has happened. They can search for evidence that it isn't true (there is probably confirmation bias at play here) in order to justify pretending that it doesn't affect them, or may attempt to displace personal discomfort by allocating blame elsewhere.

Frustration – change has still not been accepted and the individual can get angry about it to the point of trying to block or fight it.

Depression – frustration and anger have worn off but the individual exhibits low moods as they recognise what has been lost and can lose the energy or will to go on.

Experimentation – the individual begins to try out and test the new situation to some degree, to see what, if any, actions might work in the new order of things.

Decision – the individual begins to learn how the new situation works and can once again see hope enough to carry on.

Integration (to a new level) – the individual has learnt how to deal with the new situation and can do so with relative ease as well as letting go of thoughts about the old situation.

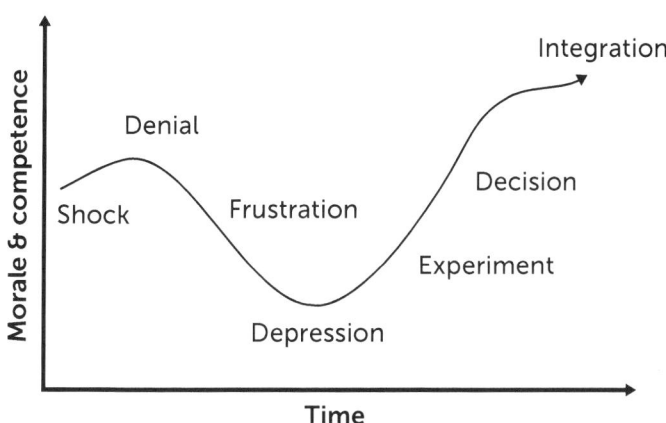

Change Curve based on the Kübler-Ross Grief Cycle

She came to believe that this was in fact a frequent model for people undergoing any kind of significant change and it's not really surprising that this link was embraced by the project management field whose aim it is to better organise and enable change; death is indeed quite a significant change, possibly one of the largest to affect those that survive it, and a pretty regular occurrence in the population at large. Culturally, there have also been associations between death and change in the rituals that surviving family members and friends undergo in most religions; even in the artistry of the Tarot deck, drawing the death card was rarely interpreted as a harbinger of death, but as a sign that change was coming (remarkably insightful mystics, take a bow).

So what can the Kübler-Ross or project management change curves tell us about how change happens and its effects on those involved? For projects, the pattern begins with activities that try to bring about an envisioned change, but soon can face such resistance (coming from our natural reaction to new things that we don't fully understand) that project progress and will to keep making it at both project team and individual levels can, if incorrectly planned or left unattended to, soon nosedive placing them into the lowest part of the curve which is called in project management parlance the 'Valley of Death' and is often the graveyard for many a well-intentioned project. This is a critical point to recognise; continued adverse reactions to the introduction of change can lead to a period of depression where hope of finding a solution evaporates. Continued effort and encouragement to just keep on going, keep making steady and continuous if only small steps towards the goal, or keep trying out new ways of dealing with the change here can help the person/team/project out of the valley into the later stages of the change curve and new levels of performance, but without it, the drop in performance (or in the original study individual's quality of life) can remain lower than before the start of the change.

In essence, the curve represents our mental state in relation to change efforts – both for individuals and the effects that change has upon groups of people faced with change.

With projects, if momentum and progress is sufficiently strangled for long enough, then the project will die as the team members lose belief that it is worth devoting any time to and deprioritise it. This is why it is important for change to be introduced to stakeholders (those upon whom it will have an effect) before it is implemented. Doing so can lessen the shock, thereby reducing the force of the rebounding resistance and the chances that this will be too great to overcome.

By involving those who are affected by the change early on before implementation occurs, you can also identify in advance the likely causes of problems or frustration, and take measures to remove them happening, or at least reduce their impact. By asking subject matter experts (frequently those who will be directly dealing with the change), you can gain valuable input into the way that the change may need to be planned and implemented for it to stand any chance of being embraced by affected stakeholders. Being a part of its development also increases the feeling among stakeholders that the change belongs to them, thereby increasing their motivation to help it succeed. And by maintaining momentum, we can help stakeholders and project teams to drive through slumps and escape the valley of death before it kills all will to continue.

Being aware of this phenomenon can help us to prepare both ourselves and others for required change, as well as being aware of what is happening to us. Understanding what stage of the curve you or others may be experiencing can help you understand steps that might need to be taken to help move through it. As we know, awareness of the need for action is the first step towards being able to take effective action.

CHANGE IS OPPORTUNITY

Bearing in mind that the world we experience is simply our perception of it, one among millions, we can now begin to view change from different points of view. Instead of seeing it simply as a strange and unknown quantity that by its very nature fills us with dread at what might be the result of its as yet unknown impact upon us (so, "it's a threat," right?) we can also look at change as the creator of opportunity.

This is true for all change, even of cataclysmic change on a global scale. The meteorite that landed in the Yucatan peninsula in our pre-history and which is thought to have caused most of the dinosaurs to become extinct was the catalyst for smaller creatures and mammals to become more widespread and it is believed was a key factor that led to our eventual appearance. New ecosystems evolved out of the changes in atmospheric conditions and surviving organisms were forced to adapt.

Coming back to the workplace, yes, change can sometimes result in things like redundancy, but if we maintain an open mind even redundancy can be viewed as an opportunity to take stock of our situation and make a new future for ourselves. It can often be the catalyst that we need to drive the change that we weren't necessarily brave enough to make on our own because the potential of trying something different was outweighed by the stability of a steady monthly income and the fear of the unknown.

At work, the vast majority of change doesn't result in redundancy, but even if it does, given the right positive mindset it can produce incredible opportunities for you to reassess where your career is headed, and provide the motivation to make the necessary changes to set it on track for where you want to go. When there is change in the marketplace, it can create new opportunities for organisations to create value for their potential customers whose needs may have changed or whose suppliers have been forced to adapt to change.

The fact is, change creates opportunity – you just need to look for it. This is such a well-recognised principle that some of the most globally dominant companies of the last 30 years have based their entire business strategy models upon it. Take Cisco for example. They pursue what's called a disruptive market strategy. While this may sound like a bad thing, it simply means that they support technological developments in certain parts of their market that will enable their target customers to gain competitive advantage. In order to adopt this technology, those companies will need to update their IT infrastructure that enables them to gain the benefits associated with being able to connect and move digitised data from one place to another – and that (IT infrastructure equipment and services) is what Cisco sells as its product offering. In a way, it's like going looking for gold, not with the objective of mining as much gold as is possible yourself, but with the goal of triggering a gold rush by making it easy for others to get rich by selling them the shovels, axes and mining supplies they will require. The opportunity for all involved is the change that allows them to get a return on their investment. In fact, a recent Cisco blog suggested that industry at large may need to consider creation of a new type of executive role, the Chief Disruption Officer, whose job would be to utilise both the IT industry and change management expertise to lead holistic strategy, action and collaboration effectively across departments, functions and partners and help organisations avoid the spectres of inertia and fear of change.

Change can also work to create opportunity on a more specific level. Imagine that you have been trying to engage a new customer, but their key decision maker, for what you believe were political reasons, did not like your company's offering. A restructure at that company could result in that person no longer being in a key decision-making role, so there may be an opportunity for you to engage with new decision makers or influencers which may give you a genuine (or improved) chance of having an objective and fair sales discussion.

Changes to the status quo can be looked at both in terms of the potential for loss that they may pose, but also in terms of the opportunities that they create. One way to do this is to conduct a SWOT analysis. If you have ever studied or done any business planning, you have probably encountered this already, but just in case I will briefly elaborate as it is useful in many ways to figure out what areas you might want to spend time focusing on in order to increase your chances of success at any given venture. In a nutshell, SWOT analysis is a simple way to look at any given situation and get some clues as to what you may need to do to succeed in achieving your goals. It asks you to identify your:

- *Strengths* – what you or your organisation are good at, in particular what you are better at than others (typically your competition). You should look at how you can best use your strengths to increase your chances of success.

- *Weaknesses* – areas where you are not so strong. You should decide if they are significant and need resolving/improving. While it would be nice to be able to eliminate these weaknesses, this is not always possible. However, weaknesses can sometimes either be downplayed, or measures taken to offer alternatives or reduce their impact so that they are not a significant problem. Understanding what your weaknesses are can also at least help you to make plans that do not rely upon your weak points.

- *Opportunities* – what aspects of the current situation (external factors independent of your capabilities) could work to your advantage? How could they be of use, whether short term or longer term?

- *Threats* – what aspects of the current situation pose significant problems to your future plans? Are there any which are real barriers to your progress, which could send it backwards or kill it off completely? Being aware of them can help you take steps to mitigate their effect or reduce the chances of them having an impact.

Both Strengths and Weaknesses are aspects of the internal capabilities of yourself or your organisation. Opportunities and Threats consider external factors, often ones that we cannot change easily such as laws, political situations or industry standards, but need to be aware of.

Carrying out this exercise once in a while helps you to take stock of your situation and gives you the chance to identify what opportunities there might be available, as well as an idea of possible actions you might take to realise them. It's also great for giving you a sense of control over your situation, and can really help you to deal with change by building a plan to manage or even drive it.

PERCEPTION IS REALITY – AND THE POWER TO CHANGE IT!

Anyone who has realised any long-term goal will tell you that quite possibly the most important thing that will govern whether or not you get there is your attitude.

From having met countless tight deadlines to being selected to play American football for my country at the unfeasibly light weight of nine stone (approx. 126lbs/57kg) I can personally vouch for that. If it's within the laws of physics, then it's do-able, as long as you are willing to put in the effort. Of course there are sometimes deep reasons why we can spur ourselves on to need to finish something, but frequently the reason why we give up, procrastinate or fail to even begin a new project is just discomfort – a feeling of being overawed by the sheer scale of what we set out to achieve. This scary sight or thought can lead us to avoid the issue in question. In reality, if we approach things correctly, then we find that we are a heck of a lot more capable than we might think.

Here's an example of how perception can colour our world and prevent us from taking action. In Malcolm Gladwell's book *Outliers: The Story of Success* he states that "researchers have settled on what they believe is the magic number for expertise: 10,000 hours"[9] (of practice). This finding may be the result of much research and hard data analysis, but because mastery or expertise are abstract words, no matter what someone else, somewhere else has defined it as, we each translate its contextual meaning in our own way. For anyone who has striven to become good at any particular discipline, in the face of this finding it is suddenly all too easy to think that to do it will take 10,000 hours for them to get really good at it. Suddenly we are faced with a mental Mount Everest to climb – will we be able to commit to such a seemingly lifelong endeavour? (At approximately 10 years per 10,000 hours, we may actually be able to fit three or four into our lives – but that would be at the expense of pretty much all of the other things we may want to do and enjoy). This thought process perturbs a lot of people from even starting ventures, unsure as to whether they could possibly ever get there.

What many don't pause to consider is that this is what it typically takes to become a master – an elite level performer. There will always be a few people out there who are driven by that all-consuming desire to be the absolute best in the world, and many more who can only wish they were. But for most of us in most of the situations we face, just getting very good or even simply competent at something is often more than enough to give us a significant enough advantage for it to have been worthwhile. So why not go for it? The likelihood is that good enough will be just that – apply yourself to any given area for any significant length of time and you will probably become quite good at it. If you then perform your skill alongside people who have not done so, then chances are you'll stand out as being significantly more able. Performing alongside others who have attained this level of skill will earn you respect as they will know the effort you have had to put in to get there. Performing alongside those who are significantly better than you gives you a great opportunity to improve by learning from and with them. What's not to like about committing to a little concerted learning?

What we often don't realise is the power that action can have on our perception. If you examine the real dynamics of learning curves, you will notice that most progress is made at the start (the law of diminishing returns kicks in more weightily the further along you go). In his book *The First 20 Hours – How To Learn Anything Fast*[10] Josh Kaufman confirms that though it may feel strange and uncomfortable, the start is where you can make great strides in your relative performance. The further you go, the smaller the improvements increments get, until by the time you reach a high level of performance, you are really just fine-tuning things. At the elite level, and especially if you are competing directly against others, small adjustments can make the difference between winning and losing. But this is a very polarised view on whether you have had any success or not. Remember our inner chimpanzee's view of life? Black or white, threat or reward, life or death. Real life is rarely like that and contains many shades of grey. So if we get a little more relative about this, we can realise that winning the top prize doesn't necessarily need to be a criterion for success.

Take a look at golfer Colin Montgomery. At the time of writing, he has never won a Major tournament, and possibly never will. But I would hardly rate his golfing career as a failure. For starters, he has regularly topped the money-earning charts for several years and has been selected for several Ryder Cup teams on the back of this, several winning ones at that. He might only be defined as a failure in that one dimension – number of Majors trophies – but for the majority of people, whether they are professional golfers or not, his career has been a roaring success. It is clear that both our definitions of success and our motivations to begin projects or tasks all hinge on our perception. As we know, there can only be one top dog, and struggling to be the best can sabotage your will to keep going if it is clear you are far from it. It can be a damaging goal. Striving to be better, however, is attainable for just about everyone, and thanks to the learning curve, considering the big gains to be made from early efforts in a new venture, you may as well get stuck in.

One thing is clear: what we achieve at work is largely is down to us making best use of the circumstances we have. We can sit around and wait for things to happen to us, or we can take it by the horns and by taking action and effecting change, make something of it that we want to happen. The motivations that govern whether or not we should begin to attempt something, keep on putting in effort to reach the goal once underway, and later on even our judgment of whether or not we have been successful, all rely on our perceptions.

And the great thing about perception is that it's rarely a constant absolute. It's a state of mind, meaning we may be able to change it quickly.

DEALING WITH CHANGE

It could be said that making progress at work simply depends upon effective change management. But what is change management? Simply put, I believe it is the combination of planning and effort involved in making people feel comfortable with change, and comfortable enough to adopt the envisaged change as a new 'normal' state. (I include ourselves as individuals in this definition of 'people'.) Granted, not all change is beneficial to us as individuals, but what if we constantly try to avoid or resist change just because it feels uncomfortable? We end up resisting pretty much all change that comes our way on principle, effectively placing ourselves at the mercy of change (remember the swirling maelstrom of change that the universe is kindly and constantly concocting for us?). Granted, there is a small chance that we may get lucky, but chances are we'll end up like the sabre-toothed tiger: a one-time top predator with no challengers overtaken by circumstance and driven to extinction when its environment changed and it no longer had the dense vegetation it needed for its ambush tactics to be effective.

There's a reason why people refer to organisations or other people who cling on to dated and ineffective methods as 'dinosaurs' – they weren't able to adapt to a rapidly changing environment either, and this principle doesn't only apply to animals. Throughout history, extremely large companies, globally renowned sports teams and even whole countries have succumbed to the folly of ignoring, trying to resist, or simply being unable to deal with change. If we rail against change when it arrives and continually fight against it, we run the risk of ending up trying to resist unstoppable forces around us that no person, animal or organisation is strong enough to overcome, eventually becoming like the sabre-toothed tiger – no longer here.

When faced with change, adaptability is the key, and assuming that as humans we are capable of taking measures to adapt to change, as we shall see later on in the chapter on learning, the first step towards feeling comfortable about change, wanting to embrace change and taking measures to be a part of and influence change is simply being aware either that change is happening, or needs to happen.

Making Change Happen

Of course, recognising that change is the natural state of the universe and therefore difficult to avoid, impossible to completely, permanently stop, and perhaps even worth exploring to feel more comfortable about, is a generalisation. What can we learn from this understanding of how we react to change in terms of making changes happen ourselves? After all, that is what work is about, for the most part: doing things that produce a desired result (a change).

In the workplace, people are the key factors in achieving change, by their intent and by their role in initiating and implementing it. In recognising how we as humans react to change, we can get better at helping other people to be less fearful of it, and make the planning and implementation of the work we have to accomplish that much less fraught with resistance. From the Kübler-Ross curve, we see that the early stages of typical reaction to change tend to be when the level of morale and motivation take a serious hit. This is partly caused by the shock of the new and unknown state of affairs, and can trigger strong emotional feelings that drive morale and hope further down towards the valley of death where so many projects lose so much momentum and support that the reason for putting any more effort or resource into them is seriously questioned, and they are frequently abandoned if not by management then by the team itself.

We now know that we can reduce the impact of the shock and the level of emotional reaction that is triggered by introducing the idea of the change required far in advance of the change being implemented. This has the benefits of giving any relevant stakeholders plenty of time to become gradually better acquainted with the change, have the chance to influence it and become a part of it, all of which improve the chances that the change will be relevant, workable and strongly supported as they have become a part of it and hopefully have a vested interest in seeing it succeed.

Rather than the shock of being forced to adapt to a change that has been imposed on them, it has already become an accepted part of how things are going to be. So before taking any actions to implement changes, try introducing people to the idea first so that you can gauge their reaction and have time to explore ways to overcome any challenges that are raised.

Doing things in this manner requires that we space out the whole process somewhat, and address each stage of the change – conceptualisation, planning, implementation and post-change embedding – in small, yet frequent steps. This is another highly useful practice to be aware of, as it offers several benefits, not least of which being the power to allow us to focus on the moment and enabling us to take the next step without worrying too much about the whole. As with the myth about being able to boil a frog by slowly increasing the heat over a long period (while dropping it straight into already boiling water will cause it to jump straight out), small incremental changes are usually far more acceptable to us as they don't seem anywhere near as shocking or difficult, and accumulated, can help us to achieve pretty large goals. Doing things in small steps also allows us the chance to keep morale up by offering many small and again, frequent opportunities to congratulate ourselves and others on each milestone, demonstrating that progress is happening (so the effort continues to be worth the time and resource invested) and helping us to maintain momentum and drive safely through the valley of death.

Start With Why

It is worth remembering that when trying to deliberately instigate change with people, whether that be oneself or others, in order for anything to happen, the people or person in question must want to change. Take a look at Alcoholics Anonymous, one of the most famous organisations in the world dedicated to helping people make and embed change. They have a specific, structured approach to helping their members change and overcome or manage their addiction to alcohol. And the very first step is acknowledging that there is a problem, that something needs to change. In business, this is often called the 'burning platform' in reference to a fictitious situation first coined by Dr. John P. Kotter,[11] internationally renowned thought leader in the fields of business, leadership and change. Kotter describes a scenario in which you are standing on a platform and are faced with a perilous jump to safety. Normally, you would have no reason to jump and risk falling, but now that the platform is burning it becomes the greater of two evils and jumping (making an effort that could result in possible death but also the possibility of survival) suddenly looks like a much more attractive proposition than a guaranteed fiery death. To make change happen, people need a good reason why and sense of urgency – what is the burning platform that will consume them if they don't take action to change things?

Understanding Why

Understanding why change is required is where every significant change effort should begin. Even if there has already been exploration of steps further along the implementation track, if there is no clear 'why', it is wise to bring the discussion back a few steps, pulling apart and exploring the reason for carrying out the proposal – what is the goal or vision, and why does that change need to happen now? The 'why' sometimes goes by other names such as Business Case or Strategic Imperative, and finding the 'why' helps us in two ways:

- It helps to define how things will look when the change has been accomplished (so you know when you have completed it and can move on to something else).

- It gives everyone involved a strong, defined reason why they should join the change effort; in business terms, it secures 'buy-in' – genuine mental commitment to want to be a part of it.

If there is no 'why' defined, people find it hard to justify committing their time and resources as there are many other important things vying for their attention, including their own and their manager's objectives. Even if they agree to volunteer some initial help, continuous requests of this type will soon wear out goodwill leading to it being deprioritised in their to do list, more so if the project is going to take some time to accomplish.

CHAPTER 1: CHANGE

The art and dynamics of understanding why is such a fundamental part of achieving goals that I believe it should be one of the fundamentals taught to everyone at school, long before we get anywhere near entering the workplace. It is present in young children who can be insatiable learners and are able to make incredible leaps of ability in just a few years thanks to the trait of persistently asking "why?" While it may sometimes feel annoying for parents, their relentless need to understand their world keeps driving them to ask why each new piece of information is so. In the workplace, we may get to a similar point with our interrogations; knowing when to stop asking why can be a useful skill. There is no absolute answer as to when this point is reached – it can vary by context, but I would suggest that your goal should be to try to get to a point of understanding how the activity or subject you are exploring contributes to the company's strategy and objectives. If you bear this in mind, then your questioning will probably be a little more concise, and you will have a good idea of when you have reached the point where further pressing is likely to return minimal gains while greatly increasing the annoyance factor for your interrogatee.

Of course, not every organisation wants people to question or challenge things; in certain workplace cultures there is a need for management to feel safe and in control by controlling the information which is available, seemingly making themselves indispensable. This may serve the short-term political wants of the people currently in control of the information, but long term it is unhealthy for most businesses and will have an effect when innovation or change is required. Staff will not feel comfortable challenging current methodologies, so achieving any change will be that much harder to do. This is of course why there is such a market for external consultancy services, as this is typically what they do for a living – explore and challenge existing methods and systems. Being outsiders, it is often safer for them to do so, as they may have been invited to do so by senior management and have not been conditioned by the existing cultural influences that surround every minute of the regular staff member's working day, plus there may be less chance that their job hinges on this single contract.

Returning to the usefulness of 'why', I have lost count of the number of times I have made a request of a work colleague and been met with some initial resistance, to find that an explanation of why this is important to me and the organisation has allowed them to feel more comfortable committing to helping me, or at least made the reception of the request that much warmer.

DON'T JUST CHANGE FOR CHANGE'S SAKE

The other thing a good 'why' does is kill off the perception that you are only trying to accomplish your goal for your own ends, or because you don't know what you are doing (or more specifically why you are doing it.) This is often the perception when people think that change is being brought about simply for its own sake: to justify a budget, or even the existence of a role or whole department simply by doing something visible and looking busy. This goes hand in hand with what one of my old managing directors described as 'rocking horse syndrome': using the illusion of movement to fool people into thinking you are being productive, when in reality you are going nowhere. It is a rare occasion where simply achieving change itself should be the only reason for doing something, and in providing a good 'why' you will be able to avoid putting effort into fruitless endeavours, and always have a better chance of getting people on board with supporting your ideas and projects.

The Techno-Trap

Structure should follow strategy, and likewise changes to organisations, systems or processes should be chosen to fit the goals, not the other way round. Technology is a classic example where many mistakes are made in this regard. Investment in new technology is often made because people think that technology on its own will drive the change required; this way of thinking is entirely the wrong way round.

While technology can aid and enable change, it is simply a tool in the change process. The driver behind change (the reason that drives everyone to make it happen) must come from somewhere else – the 'why'. This point is often missed as people are dazzled by new capabilities and gimmicks that promise a new, utopian way of working and that simply getting new technology is enough of a reason for people to use it and change processes. It is not uncommon to see technologies being deployed which no one adopts or uses as the people expected to use it have been given no reason to change current habits, and so quickly reject the new system, resist it, or soon give up on efforts to overcome initial glitches and make it work choosing to stick with the comfort of what is a known quantity – the old way of doing things. As we have seen, unless we can see evidence to the contrary, change or difference tends to be treated as a threat.

A Practical Guide To Technological Change

I am picking on technology not because I am a Luddite, but because the availability of new technology is so ubiquitous that there are plenty of opportunities to fall into the change techno-trap, and I have seen it to be a widespread problem, with some organisations making the same mistake time and time again. This is why I feel it will be highly relevant to many of the people reading this book. So here are a few practical steps to help avoid misplaced investment:

- Before deciding on a new system, first understand your existing business processes and how they really work. It's surprising how many organisations are out of touch with this, either because they have left it so long since the last time they examined their own processes that their business needs have changed, or because they have never questioned their processes since they were created. Process mapping can help here, as being able to see the process makes it easier to see the dynamic effects they are having.

- Next decide how things should/could be in an ideal world, and why this would be so.

- Then look for workable solutions that can enable some, or all, of the ideal scenario, deciding which elements you can and will change within the limits of your resources.

- You will now have a reason for change, plus a rough plan as to what changes are needed. This is a good point at which you may now wish to explore the technological options that could help you to attain the goals you have set, as you will now have a better understanding of what types of technology (if any is required) will support your objective and strategy (good business sense). From there you can refine the details of which of the available options in the market would be a good fit for your exact needs.

I have worked for companies that followed this process, in one instance deploying a company-wide Enterprise Resource Planning system extremely smoothly. When other companies in our group adopted the system, they found implementation extremely difficult and costly, as they didn't follow this process sufficiently, resulting in costly workarounds later in the process when many fundamental parameters had been incorrectly set in stone.

I have also worked with companies who didn't understand why a technical solution built for one market wasn't effective in another. They didn't put the time into understanding these other markets and their different processes before they made the decision to roll out the technology to them. The lesson? Spend some time understanding the context before deciding what type of technology or change you may need to implement, or even if you need to implement any at all at this point.

PLANNING *VS* EXECUTION?

When implementing change, I have frequently been asked and been involved in debates about which is the most important: planning or execution? Well, there's a reason why I have titled this sub-chapter in such a manner. Often, people discuss this as if the two are mutually exclusive elements where only one can exist or the other.

There are many different outlooks on this question, each of which can vary by industry, context or experience. Some industries, for example, allow for ongoing development or rework as part of their natural development process. Software is a good example of this, with different versions of applications being released on a continuous basis, with new patches to resolve bugs or enable new capabilities developed on the fly as the intricate web of complexity grows ever wider. Some performance is sacrificed at the expense of progress. This could be used to argue that execution is essential to change, making it the more important of the two.

However, there are also industries in which progress must be held back until the relevant stakeholders are satisfied that incredibly stringent performance levels can be met by every single component and process involved. Aerospace is a good example of this: if things go wrong, there could potentially be billions of dollars on the line or worse, human life itself. This might support the argument that in these situations planning is all-important, or great human catastrophe may happen.

So we still have no clear answer, but we may be able to get closer by looking at a theoretical example, which takes usage of each to the extreme.

The Value Of Planning

Why plan? Simply put, to decide where we need to go (which often requires figuring out where we are now) and get an idea of what needs to happen in terms of organising resources and circumstances in order to get us there. Without it, we are destined to rely upon luck that we got everything right. While chaos theory supports the notion that given enough time, an infinite number of monkeys with an infinite number of word processors and power could, by pure chance, eventually reproduce the complete works of Shakespeare, in reality, nobody has infinite resources, especially not time. Surely this makes planning more important than action, right?

Well, it does give you a structure. Good for people who like and need to have some recognised process, having a structure allows anyone involved to see more easily what is required and why, enabling them to align their efforts more easily in the right direction. Even if your plan has flaws (relax, it will, nothing's perfect), having written it down, we now have a logged reference that makes it easier for us to analyse and know which parts may need to be changed, or post-project, easier for us to learn about what could be improved. Human memory is notoriously unreliable over time, and our capacity for conscious thought is limited and quickly tires out, so writing things down helps greatly reduce the burden on our minds of recalling all of the information we may need, plus it improves the accuracy of recall.

Detailed planning can be good, but beware of one caveat: the generation of too many options can lead to paralysis by analysis, where we have so many choices to deal with that we can't make up our minds which way to go. To avoid this situation, keep things simple and build yourself a plan that you can start to execute quickly. Hmmm, suddenly planning, while still important, doesn't seem to be the be-all and end-all any more, does it?

In the absence of a plan, remember any plan is better than none, as it allows us to mentally check the box that at least some even if only rudimentary thought has gone into understanding why we are doing something and how we should do it, giving us a mental 'green light' and allowing us to move to the next stage – execution. While we know that we may have to revise some parts of our plan as we learn more about our task, progress has been enabled, and we won't mentally prevent ourselves from taking the next step due to the gnawing worry that we are building with no foundations, or are doing things without knowing why.

There are many idioms which while general in nature, illustrate the value of planning:

"One hour of planning saves 10 of execution."

"Fail to prepare, prepare to fail."

And lastly, a version originating from the military called the 7 Ps from which I have removed one P on the grounds of common decency, though the message remains the same:

"Proper planning and preparation prevents poor performance."

What they are all saying is that planning helps to improve performance and reduces the amount of resources we may waste on trial and error techniques or last-minute scrambles which expose us to the laws of supply and demand (meaning things get more expensive, if they are possible at all at short notice). Being able to avoid such pitfalls is a highly useful skillset at work where resources are usually limited by budgets, availability or deadlines.

The Value Of Execution

So do our findings this far suggest that planning is the more important of the two? It can after all save a lot of randomly aimed effort and resource, both critical to companies or individuals desiring long-term survival. But all of the planning in the world is worth nothing without action. In the words of futurist and author Joel A. Barker, "Vision without action is merely a dream." Having a plan and never acting on it, we are guaranteed never to achieve our ends. Action can always accomplish *something*, but as we have seen, if there is no plan then there is a miniscule chance of getting it right and achieving what we intended, and if we somehow do so, it will likely have been at excessive, possibly prohibitive cost. So, which is more important? In theory, assuming you achieve something, then execution may technically have the edge – you at least have a chance of reaching your goal, miniscule as it may be, but you're going to need a lot of luck, resources or both.

As with so many apparent dichotomies, in asking the question, "This one, or that one?" we fall into the polarisation trap, the extremism of assuming that the only two answers offered by the question are the only two possible answers. The smart answer, which takes account of the reality of our workplaces, is illustrated by Mr. Barker's expanded quote:

"Vision without action is merely a dream. Action without vision just passes the time. Vision with action can change the world."[12]

Both are vital to progress. Practically, the planning element can often be condensed into a simple checklist, which (assuming we already have a valid 'why') can be built by asking a short series of questions, such as:

- What do we need to do to make this happen?

- Are we able to do this?

- Are there any obstacles in our way?

- Who will do it and when will they have it completed by?

- Is there anything else to consider?

In thinking of the two as somehow competing with one another, we miss out on truly understanding their combined value when used together. Different circumstances will need varying degrees of each discipline, but the lesson here is that you should not be focused on one to the complete exclusion of the other. I hope you can now see why we must not fall foul of putting these two at opposite ends of a spectrum, but instead view them as complementary disciplines.

As I mentioned in the introduction, taking things to absolutes can be useful for theoretical exploration, but when dealing with the practicalities of the real world doing so is rarely a sustainable strategy. Using only one methodology or taking only one viewpoint severely limits our capabilities and, like the sabre-toothed tiger, puts us in danger of being rendered ineffective when circumstance requires that we find a different way.

Persistence

I feel an important point to make regarding execution is one of its fundamental rules: if you want to get anywhere, at some point you will need to start taking action, then (and this is where many well-intentioned plans fall down) keep at it! It sounds glaringly obvious, but in the era of quick fixes, hedonistic distractions and myriad choices, we can soon find ourselves surrounded by a host of well-intentioned plans that once begun, never got finished. Further to that, the stresses of achieving something that takes time to develop can have a serious effect on our will to want to continue with the tasks required.

I would like you to remember firstly the following phrase, and the considerations that follow:

> *When projects hit rocky patches or difficult obstacles, some days will feel like the end of the world.*

Yes, things will go wrong, perhaps several things at the same time, and you may be tired and finding it more difficult to deal with multiple stress sources. One of the best pieces of advice I have received in these situations is to keep going simply by taking some kind of action – do *something*, *anything* that helps keep your progress ticking over, no matter how small. (I find it also helps to focus your mind on something other than worrying.) Remember your 'why', and that the majority of obstacles can be overcome with consistent, persistent effort.

Several keys to being able to motivate yourself to take another step and drive through the feelings of despair lie in the statement itself, and this is why I wanted you to remember it, so let's pull it apart.

'*Some days*' – when you hit those difficult patches, you can use labelling to remember that this feeling is only a temporary state of mind. It will not last forever, and there will be better days, so there is always hope which comes from the knowledge that things can and generally with the application of effort, will get better.

Secondly, the word '*feel*' is also pertinent as it shows this is simply the way you are perceiving the situation right now. Recognising that this is a feeling, or a perception, we now also know that sometimes with nothing more than a little sleep to improve our mood and objectivity, it can be changed. So we have another ray of light at the end of the tunnel.

Finally, let's deal with '*the end of the world*.' In all honesty, however bad things may feel at a certain point in time, nothing short of death itself is really the end of anybody's world, is it? In almost every case, no way, no how. Take a look at the news. Every day you will find examples of people in excruciatingly bad circumstances. People suffering from debilitating illness, people who are caught in the middle of war zones, people who have lost limbs and livelihoods. As long as they are still alive, they keep going. Doing whatever they can with whatever they've got to survive and rebuild. This is not intended to be a simplistic, easy fix, "Chin up," cure-all maxim. It is meant to illustrate just how incredibly inspiring the strength of the human spirit can be, something that perhaps can give many of us some perspective and indeed hope that our circumstance is not as truly awful as our initial reactions to it make out, and that even if it is, there is almost always opportunity for us to do something to improve our situation or feelings about it.

"Inaction breeds doubt and fear. Action breeds confidence and courage. If you want to conquer fear, do not sit at home and think about it. Go out and get busy."[13]

Dale Carnegie

It's incredible how putting in some effort and seeing even small results can help us to get over initial emotional reactions and realise that things can get better. This self-generated hope can help us to drive through incredible challenges and adversity. If you have ever pushed yourself physically, you may recognise the burst of motivation to try the next level of challenge that kicks in once you pass your first milestone. For me, this was never more evident than when I had to train for an adventure race which required endurance conditioning for mountain biking, canoeing and running up and down mountainous terrain for the best part of two and a half days. I had always to that point been a ball sports type of person – give me a visible target to hunt down and I was happy – I could work in intense short bursts for a couple of hours at a time. But consistent endurance? Not my thing, I got bored and demotivated by the constant pain at what seemed like a never-ending effort. So I started with a single mile. Once I got through this a few times, I moved up to five kilometres. I soon made it through my first 5K and realised that I was making fast progress, and actually enjoying it as I had moved through the initial doubts of the learning cycle and into a place where I knew I could make more progress. The pain from pushing myself was still there, but I was able to enjoy it, or at least appreciate it as an indicator that I was pushing myself to the next level. That ability to enjoy the pain came from not worrying about whether I could do it or not; I was just going out and doing what I could, and noticing my progress as a result.

So, in being able to step outside of the feeling itself for a moment and observing what's going on, acknowledging that a bad day is caused by a feeling, and (as if I haven't laboured the point enough) that this is simply a transient state of mind, we can suddenly get our ray of hope. We are aware of the issue and able to try and figure out what we might be able to do about it – we have passed through the first stage of implementing change, that of being aware that there is an issue or opportunity.

MORE MINDSET MAINTENANCE

So, what other ways are there of managing our attitude and maintaining a positive approach to change? This question alone has given rise to countless psychology and self-help books, texts and research papers, and the field itself is still relatively new in terms of our 'maturity of understanding' of it. In the interests of practicality, I would like to share with you a few tips that I have found work for me.

When I have a mood challenge, I often find writing to be an incredibly cathartic activity. Why does this work? Perhaps because it allows us to voice our fears and concerns. It might seem strange that making them more solid and more real would help us to overcome them. In fact, wouldn't that actually make them scarier? Perhaps, but I have found that it also has several other, much more useful and more significant effects (you will see several of them surface throughout the book, each time I refer to 'the power of writing things down'). On the one hand, it can help us to feel that we have expressed our feelings – to whom? Well, I'm not sure that it even really matters. Even if I don't send what I write to anyone else, or use it for anything after I have written it down or typed it, it is almost as if just in the act of creation I have shared it with the world. This in itself gives me a sense of hope that something can be done about it, and that someone else in the world now stands a better chance of seeing my problem and understanding it or possibly coming up with a solution to it that I couldn't. I feel as though I've taken a step towards enabling the power of the 'hive mind'.

In not only describing the situation, but also including a description of how it makes me feel, I have also shared (with the world outside of my own head) a piece of my inner self – making me feel like I am a little closer to something larger than myself – in this case possibly the world at large, or even the universe. While this sounds like I may be getting a little too 'new agey', I originally began with the intention of merely describing the effect that I have consistently found writing to have upon my mood so that others may try it out, but upon reading around the subject I found that this theory does have some scientific research backing it up. In his book *The Happiness Hypothesis* Jonathan Haidt describes how the desire to belong, and the effect of feeling like we belong to something bigger than ourselves (i.e. transcending our own self) is one of the fundamental factors that influences our daily happiness level in a lasting and sustainable way.[14] Short-term hits from superficial pleasures such as accumulation of wealth or drugs, when experienced on a regular basis, require continual exponential intensity to hit the same levels of feeling and satisfaction.

Transcendence doesn't work in this way, instead providing a more consistent feel-good effect, which doesn't fall victim to the law of diminishing returns as readily. Writing the issue down also allows us to define and indeed limit our worries about it, making the task of managing them seem that much easier or achievable. It also allows us to view the shape, structure and dynamics of the problem more objectively. We have taken a step towards giving ourselves back a sense of having some control over our lives, something which when lacking is widely held to be a major cause of anxiety.

This feeling of control is reinforced not only because we have given a shape and form to the source of our anxiety, but also because in doing so we have slowed things down (our minds cannot race as fast due to the fact that we cannot speak or write as fast as we can think) and removed a good deal of what it is not (the lightning-fast worst case scenario reactions that our minds use to fill in knowledge gaps).

ELIMINATION

Elimination can also be a useful tool when having to make choices. In essence, elimination helps us to choose where we focus our attention. When we are able to do that, we can gain great insight, perform more effectively, and make faster progress.

Things that stop us from focusing our attention include anxiety caused by worry; whether these are direct issues or situational ones that we can see coming in the future, we spend a part of our conscious processing power trying to deal with them, thus diluting the amount of attention or thought power we can devote to any one of them.

There is a good example of this happening right now, as I draft this chapter in my local coffee shop. This light, relaxed and welcoming atmosphere was briefly switched to one of a potential danger situation as somebody dropped and smashed a load of crockery that had just come out of the dishwasher. It being behind me probably exacerbated this feeling, but my mind was for a second switched into defensive mode by the shock, and the flowing train of thought that I was in dried up as my limbic system swung into action in case I needed protecting. As it was, I soon recognised that there was no threat as such, and was able to get back into the flow state by slowing down my breathing to help me relax again.

If we can eliminate or reduce the feelings of anxiety we feel from other issues that face us, then we can free up mental effort to focus more wholly on the things we want to which can help us progress. Instead, and all too frequently, our propensity to notice difference and classify it as a threat by default leads us to worry, often unnecessarily, about a great many things which are either beyond our control, or not really significant problems. The problem is, in the absence of hard evidence our minds turn these things over and over, looking for the worst case scenario (so that we can be ready for it, thus prolonging our survival), and creating stories to justify our self-protective behaviour.

In just noticing that this is what typically happens, it gives us a chance to deal with it and increase our chance of being able to focus our attention better on what matters. When we write down our description of what is actually happening, and what we feel, we are able to analyse more clearly and see the real extent of the problem, if there is any at all. The process of logging the information allows our brains to make reference to it more easily in our mental evaluation, and allows us to focus more attention on analysing the actual relationships rather than trying to do that while juggling the reference materials/reference points in our minds at the same time. It's the same principle that makes writing things down in meetings on whiteboards such an effective technique for helping us to analyse things and make decisions more easily. Consider it to be a mental parking lot for the information that needs to be driven into and out of the analysis.

SUMMARY

- Change is inevitable and ubiquitous and we deal with much of it very well.

- Our brains treat too much or too sudden a change as a threat; a default reaction to 'keep us safe'.

- Recognising this happening gives us the chance to manage our reactions: labelling and reappraising the situation are two useful methods.

- Early involvement in envisioned change can help to regulate negative reactions in us and in others.

- Change creates opportunity; changing our perception can help us see it.

- When planning change, start with 'why?'

CHAPTER 2
COMMUNICATION

Like change, another factor that is so ubiquitous, so pervasive, so fundamental to our working lives that it lies at the core of most of the other chapters is communication. And because of its ubiquity, it is also one of the factors that we all too easily forget to develop and practise effectively; because we are communicating constantly we often neglect to put effort into getting better at doing so.

One of the standout factors in our evolutionary journey was the ability to communicate ever more effectively. Communication allows us to work together. It allows us to build communities and leverage the benefits of group effort. It allows us to define new ideas and abstract concepts, pass on information and learnings and drive the future progress of ourselves and others, even long after we as individuals have gone. In an evolutionary context it is one of the chief reasons that we are where we are today, and if we were getting a bit more metaphysical in our description, we could think of it in a similar way to how The Force is described by Obi-Wan Kenobi in Star Wars[15] – an invisible fabric that binds together and influences our societies, cultures, routines and pretty much everything that we do. Except that wouldn't be wholly correct.

Much of the evidence of how we communicate is extremely visible, audible, smellable, touchable or otherwise easy to perceive in some way. Because the evolutionary advantages of doing so are so great, we are built to communicate. On top of languages and awareness of how we communicate and its effects, we have developed an incredible array of tools and continue to develop new ways in which to use them more effectively to meet our needs.

Later on we will look in more detail about the intent of our ends and how that can have an effect upon the effectiveness of the methods we choose; but in how we choose to communicate and the different options available to us, we have the crux of this chapter.

We'll take a look at the basic elements of communication, the dynamics of how they interact, and what this means to us if we want to be able to use them effectively.

WHEN THERE IS NO COMMUNICATION

But before we get into the process, I'd like to make a very important point. Getting better at communicating, achieving progress through effective communication is based upon the assumption that there is communication happening. Sometimes, however, it can break down or stop, usually because we have chosen to stop communicating (often the net result of toxic or poor communication), sometimes because it has been suppressed, but often because we have forgotten how important it is to keep doing so.

Most, if not all of the greatest human accomplishments in history have relied upon communication. Some of the greatest tragedies in human history have been the result of a lack of effective communication, or deliberate attempts to prevent it or use it for the wrong purposes.

What happens when there is no communication? Looking back to the chapter on change, we fill in the information gaps we may have with our own stories or interpretations of events. We need to do this to be able to make decisions. And when left to themselves with no evidence to suggest otherwise, our brains tend to err on the negative side, imagining the worst (that anything new could be a potential threat) and preparing us for it – fight, flight or freeze. So these stories and assumptions become the base for our map of the world and each subsequent decision reinforces our assumptions unless we find new evidence. If there is no communication, there is a high chance that we will not receive as much new evidence that could convince us to question our assumptions, so we get more and more convinced that our thinking is the truth, making any change or adjustment in viewpoint that might be required more difficult.

Many groups through history have attempted to manipulate this principle to their own selfish ends, from the Nazis who in World War II burned books to try and remove physical evidence of views that conflicted with their own, to dictators who try to suppress even discussion on some topics by rule of fear and extreme threat, to ancient rulers who destroyed all evidence of cultures they conquered in an attempt to erase completely from history the fact that they had ever existed.

Absence of open communication is not only responsible for the mobilisation of large groups into committing sometimes horrific acts, but also for unhappiness at an individual relationship level as countless marriage counsellors will testify. At a situation specific level, there may be times when more or less communication suits, but at a general ongoing level, I would simply echo the sentiments of Professor Stephen Hawking that in order for mankind to continue to survive and progress, we have the capacity do so – as long as we keep on talking to one another.

Understanding better the components and dynamics of how communication happens is how we can tune up our skills and make ourselves shine as effective communicators – something that every workplace has desperate need of if it is to thrive or even just survive, and an ability that employers value and colleagues appreciate.

SOME KEY ELEMENTS OF EFFECTIVE COMMUNICATION

While communication formats have proliferated over the last few years with the advent of instant messaging, texting, blogs, vlogs and countless other ways of communicating, the basic principles of the communications process are present in each piece of communication.

The sender originates an idea that they encode into a message, which is sent via a chosen communication method (medium) to the receiver (or audience) who must then decode the meaning and decide whether or not they will choose to respond or take action.

Each of these elements has its own particular set of dynamics and can have a profound effect on the whole communication process, as does the context within which the communication occurs. Understanding more about each can greatly improve the chances that your communications will be effective, so let's take a deeper look.

Sender

On one side of any communication, we have the person or organisation sending the message who is trying to achieve a particular objective. Much of their success will be dictated by the intent of their objective, as this can have a big effect on whether the recipient is open to listening to it. In the context of becoming an effective communicator, you may view yourself as the sender each time, but we can gain tremendous insight if we were to examine how we perceive those who try to send messages to us. What sort of questions do we typically ask ourselves about those who try to communicate with us? They could include:

- Why are they sending this message/what is their context?

- Can I trust them?

- If I'm not sure, what might need to happen for me to feel comfortable doing so?

So, as we can see there are a lot of contextual factors that can come into play for anyone to even consider listening to any communication. Thinking about a communication from both the points of view of the sender and the recipient(s) can greatly enhance the effectiveness of a communication, as it increases the chances that it will be relevant and acceptable to the recipient, and therefore paid attention to. As an experiment to illustrate how relevancy works, (and if you're brave enough to try) see what happens if you shout a random name across a busy room. As most of those people won't share that name, they won't respond — it is largely irrelevant to them. If you shout the name of somebody in the room, there's a very good chance they will respond. Hey presto, relevance in action (you've also just generated a great opportunity to make a new friend/get some practice at thinking on your feet!).

Audience

Consider their context and capacity: why should they listen to or pay any attention to your communication? What's in it for them? Useful information? Demonstrable return? Banking of social credit or favours that could be drawn upon at a later date?

The way in which the recipient decodes and translates the meaning of your message is unfortunately entirely in their hands and highly subject to factors such as their experiences, mental outlook and view of the world, even how they are feeling at the time. Be aware that even the most well-crafted communications can be subject to this personally individualised treatment.

Also be aware of who your audience should be and also could be. If you 'Reply All' to an email, then everyone that email was originally sent to is going to see your reply. Should they be included, or would your response be better continued as a private conversation? It can be tempting to copy everyone to garner moral support or to make yourself appear or feel clever, but it can also cause embarrassment to the person to whom you are talking if you are sharing a critical opinion. If there's one thing that will almost certainly provoke an angry response instead of consideration of an opportunity to discuss or learn, it's public shame.

So before automatically replying to all, consider whether your response is going to help the whole group, or annoy some of them as it will be an irrelevant interruption to their efforts to concentrate on their job and would be better if continued on a more personal level. It's not uncommon for an initial light-hearted comment on a widely circulated internal email to trigger several off-the-cuff responses that while not offending anyone, escalate to a level whereby the group receives a polite (or in some cases less than polite) reprimand from either a senior manager or HR reminding everyone that such conversations are more suitable for private exchanges and personal (i.e. non-paid) time. Remember, everybody wants to be a comedian… except the boss.

And just as technology is making it easier for rapid transmission of written communications, so it also changes the potential dynamic of anything you send to someone else. It is incredibly easy for a private discussion to be shared outside of the expected audience and suddenly become open to the rest of the world to comment on in public forums, so take care about what you send out and try to be as professional as you can at all times.

The Curse Of Knowledge

Recognising the level of understanding of your audience is also important in terms of crafting the right kind of message for them. Think about whether they will understand any jargon or acronyms before using them. If you're unsure, it's best to explain each time adding the acronym in brackets for future reference. The tendency to speak in terms beyond the understanding of your audience (without realising it) is an incredibly easy one to fall foul of, and has its own name: the curse of knowledge. Like the difficulty someone who can ride a bike has in recognising how it felt to not be able to ride the bike, the curse of knowledge makes it extremely difficult for subject matter experts to recognise that certain aspects of their message may not be known to the audience, due to the fact that, for them, this knowledge is now second nature. While it's difficult to ever completely overcome this cognitive bias (assuming your audience knows as much as you expect), just being aware of it can help reduce the chances of it becoming too much of an issue.

Sometimes it can help to have someone outside of your industry or topical area to give you their feedback on whether they can understand your message. This can give you a pointer as to whether the curse of knowledge might be likely to affect your communication.

If you have the opportunity, verify with your audience certain expected understandings before you begin your communication. It's worth noting that if you ask people in a group whether or not they understand something, especially in the workplace, the pressure they perceive in being expected to be competent at their job can lead them simply to confirm they do understand even if they don't, like the courtiers in the story of the Emperor's New Clothes. So you could even bypass the opportunity for this to happen by offering a summarised explanation of anything you feel may be even slightly beyond generally accepted understanding. It may be worth stating and underlining the fact that it's OK to ask questions. And to check that they are still with you, certainly for verbal communications, it may be worth asking for confirmation that what you are saying makes sense, making it safe for them to ask you to elaborate on any of the points that may not have been understood.

Medium

The medium you choose for each communication is also of great importance. It is one of the more mechanical aspects of whether or not your audience will pay attention to your message. In fact, it could be a deciding influence on whether your audience are even capable of paying attention to your message. There's an old situational joke that goes some way towards illustrating this point:

> John: "Did I tell you I was talking with Tony in America last night?"
>
> John's Mum: "What, on the phone?"
>
> John (extremely sarcastically): "No... we were shouting."

The lesson here being that any medium you choose has to be at the very least physically capable of getting the message across to the recipient. In today's cosmopolitan world, we also have to consider factors like language barriers, differences in cultural meaning, and of course ease of use on the parts of both recipient and sender. You will need to consider what media are possible options in terms of effectiveness, but also in terms of return on cost, time and effort required, and, as with composing your message, you must also consider your audience in terms of which of these would be acceptable to them and whether or not they have any particular preference.

With this in mind, let's have a look at some of the strengths and weaknesses of some core communication mediums. While new technologies continue to blend and blur the lines between traditional formats, enabling each to share the strengths of the others, I would like to focus on two of them in particular and some of the typical ways in which they might be used.

Written (Physically or Digitally)

- Pros – It has lasting presence. From a message in a bottle to the categories in a filing system, you can give copies to people to refer to later or leave written communications in places where you are not and it has the capacity to continue giving out a message whether you are there or not.

- Cons – Traditional forms (physical material, whether written or printed) are a fairly static, non-dynamic, fixed format which are costly and time consuming to change or reproduce, certainly so when compared to verbal communications. Physical material can also have a significant transportation cost, and is limited by this dependence on its physical presence – each piece can only be in one place at a time.

    One of its strengths – longevity of presence (i.e. it can be left alone, whether with someone or in a given place and can continue delivering its message – useful for reminders or memory jogging) can also be detrimental if the wrong message is put out into the world. This latter point applies equally, if not especially, to online material. Thanks to its ethereal nature, it overcomes many of the physical limitations of physically recorded material, but is so easy to share that copies can proliferate around the entire world in minutes and stay there for a long time, making it nigh on impossible to fully erase once out there.

CHAPTER 2: COMMUNICATION

Bearing in mind the effect of written communication in the workplace, it is worth paying close attention to the naming conventions that you use, especially for digital filenames and folders. If you're saving work, have a think about how that file is going to be found in the future. Make it easy for yourself and for other people to remember – people who will not necessarily share your knowledge or memories about the nature or content of the file, or think in the way that you do. Make it as easy and obvious as you can for you and your audience to understand quickly what is inside the file from its title. Instead of accepting system-generated filenames (e.g. file 0000316.jpg or 2014_3_000316.jpg) you may wish to rename files, or when originating them yourself, include some keywords about the topic and the function of the file, e.g. Marketing Strategy Plan 2014, or London XYZ trade show product presentation 2015.

This applies equally to designing structures that will hold information which other people may need to access. How do you think they are likely to try and search for what they want? An IT person may build a navigation structure for a public-facing website that makes sense to them and other IT people, but which is so industry-specific jargon heavy that the users do not have the knowledge required to understand how they should use it. Try to make your written communications and structures intuitive and obvious for those who will need to use them. I call this the Ronseal technique, after the UK manufacturer of garden and wood care products who has become synonymous with the slogan they first began using in 1994, and which has now entered common parlance for something which is as it appears without the need for further explanation: "It does exactly what it says on the tin."

Here's another workplace housekeeping tip that will save you a lot of hassle and others will thank you for it: understanding version control. If you are developing a file and need to share it with someone to review, if you happen to have to send it or make it available to them for review, give the file you send them a version reference number, for example at the end of the filename. So, for example, Marketing Strategy 2014 v2. With files that are subject to frequent change during their development, this will allow anyone talking about the file to know instantly which version they are talking about. It will also allow you to keep track of what comments or changes were made to which file. One of the most annoying aspects of working together with someone else is when they aren't organised enough to know what they are doing; not knowing what materials or resources they are working on or referring to is a communication killer in this regard, and with the application of a simple, yet highly effective habit, you can instantly banish much of the confusion and organise your work and interactions with others more effectively.

Oral

- Pros – A highly dynamic format, adaptable to changing situations almost as fast as we can think. Oral dialogue can quickly and easily be adjusted using tone, speed and amplitude, allowing conveyance of a lot more contextual information than the mere words.

- Cons – Unless recorded, it is transient, disappearing almost as soon as it has been communicated, and therefore more difficult for the audience to remember over longer periods of time if not reinforced. Even when recorded, it is not immediately obvious that it even exists unless being broadcast or highlighted by another format.

When the Medium Doesn't Fit

Be aware that communication is a dynamic and live entity; because of the incredible variety of methods available to us, and the almost infinite variability in tone and meaning that can develop over the course of the simplest conversation, we should be ready to change the format to suit the changing dynamic of any communication. As with progress at large, agility lies at the core of being consistently effective.

From automated telephone systems that have been dumped into customer service processes without much thought as to the actual user experience, to staff who wonder why simply verbally telling their colleagues about a new process didn't seem to have much of an impact in terms of changing their behaviour, format can have a damaging effect on communication objectives if no thought is given to it.

CHAPTER 2: COMMUNICATION

A great example of how choosing a poor medium impacts upon daily work life is what I call 'email wars' – an extremely common phenomenon in some of the working environments I have experienced. Email wars happen when the recipient misunderstands the tone or meaning of an email communication to such a degree that they feel it is a personal attack. Thus, their fight or flight mechanism takes over. Due to the fact that it is not as immediate a threat to safety as face-to face disagreement, this often results in the decision to fight – from behind the safety of the keyboard. A highly emotional, sarcastic or passively aggressive response is written, and sent to the sender of the original message which caused the reaction. The same pattern then repeats itself when the original sender reads the 'counter attack' and feels threatened themselves. This vicious circle has the capacity to spiral quickly into a tit-for-tat exchange of wordy, pointless one-upmanship. Because it is conducted in such an impersonal way (even knowing who the audience is, when at the end of a network connection it doesn't take much prompting for them to become a faceless enemy), it is easy to forget that the other party is a person with feelings and the capacity to be offended, so the humanistic angle is often outweighed by the temptation to defend our standpoint and reputation, and 'fight on'.

The problem stems from email being a particularly poor medium to use when trying to convey nuances of meaning or tone of voice. When people know each other well, this can be done because the receiver and sender have a common understanding of intent and a wide range of expected reasons why the communication needn't necessarily be construed as a personal attack. But without that established understanding, and sometimes even with it, misunderstanding of the tone of the message is easy when there are no other contextual cues, visual or otherwise, to go on.

Having been involved in and having observed a great many of these situations over the length of my career, I have come to the conclusion that apart from highlighting an area of possible disagreement that requires further discussion, they do little more than breed contempt between the recipients once the first volley has been fired. Post-conflagration, the involved parties frequently find out that they actually agreed about the core issue and the disagreement was nothing more than reaction to a misunderstood or unintended nuance.

So, how to handle them? Very simply, talking (with your voice!). If you can't do it in person, then get on the phone or Skype or some other way in which you can get a real feel for the actual tone and intention behind the communications being sent. Even if you have travelled a long way down the apparent 'road to victory' against your 'opponent', talking is the best way to reframe what is happening and encourage open and objective resolution.

Trust me on this, I have even tried to make apologies and objectively explain what I felt was happening in the situation via a return email, but without the ability to convey the exact tone and genuine sincerity, intent and sense of contrition I felt, my explanation was met with much the same sense of indignation as the initial email exchanges. Once you reach this stage, textual format alone just can't do justice to the level of personal engagement required for these sensitive conversations.

If you find yourself in one of these situations and the nature of the response you have received makes you feel so strongly that you need to respond strongly in some way, looking back to the section on emotional regulation, learn to recognise that it is just a feeling, and that it will pass. In the moment, your urge may be to strike back immediately, so one way to buy yourself enough time for your limbic system to calm down is to write a reply, but on two strict conditions:

- **Condition Number 1**: Make a promise to yourself never to send it. Write it out, and leave it for 30 minutes or longer if necessary, even if it's with a mind to adjust the draft at a later time to make it more of a perfect riposte.

- **Condition Number 2**: To ensure you uphold Condition Number 1, before you begin to write it, delete all names from the send to and cc fields. This eliminates the chances of you falling foul of automatically clicking 'Send' out of habit, instead of closing or deleting it.

When you write out the reply, get down the essence of what you were originally trying to communicate and why you feel the way you do. This simple action brings into play one of the benefits stemming from the power of writing things down. Giving a voice to your thoughts and feelings gives you back a sense of control over the situation, even if you don't send the email. Writing them down also helps to define (and therefore limit) them and make your likely response much more coherent. It also slows down your thought process, and in drafting then leaving your response for review later, gives you enough time to review it with an entirely fresh, more objective, and hopefully less emotionally overstimulated point of view.

Once you have drafted your email, left it for a while and returned to it, then is a good time to either redraft your message into something that is going to help you both deal with the situation, or delete the message. In either instance, if you haven't done so already, this is a good time to get on the phone to the person in question (in private if necessary to spare everyone's blushes), or if you can, speak to them in person. Again, this should be in private if at all possible, as there will be less tendency on both your parts to feel like you need to be publicly proven right, leading to more candid, honest and objective discussion.

If necessary, apologise for what you may have already said, and be prepared to explain exactly and objectively what you were trying to communicate at the start, minus the added vitriol that was doubtlessly added to try and help you prove that you were right. Keep objectivity at the front of your mind, as you may have to endure the other person explaining why what you wrote wound them up so much. The safety of a private means of resolving the issue is the platform required to open conciliatory dialogue, the sincerity of your intent to mutually explore and resolve the issue, the key to keeping it going.

This doesn't mean that you shouldn't use email formats to communicate as much, it just means you should be aware of the format's capacity to cause conflict easily in the modern office. When you sense an email war about to begin, hopefully you can now avoid automatically responding to the trigger to fight fire with fire, and take an objective view on what you might need to do to avoid that escalation, saving many people a lot of time and needless loss of trust or respect.

Message

Reviewing some fundamental aspects of developing your message, I would suggest that foremost among them should be knowing what your objective is, and shaping your intent. While they may appear to be the same thing, they differ in subtle ways. Having a clear objective will help you to make a lot of the other decisions about how you build your communication, giving you the logical reasons why. You may need to ask yourself what effect you are trying to elicit from your audience: are you communicating to inform them of something, merely make them aware of something, or do you want to trigger some kind of action on their part? If so, make sure you express your call to action sufficiently well.

Your intent focuses more on the moral imperative for it. Is your intent to deceive your audience for your own ends, or is it done with mutual benefit in mind? This factor itself can have a profound effect on the way in which you build your communication and content, whether you realise it or not at the time. Humans are quite good at subconsciously noticing tiny inconsistencies between professed intent and actual behaviour, so unless your intent is congruent with your communication, there's a good chance you will set off the threat reaction in your audience, causing them to reject, avoid or even fight your message. Even if people do not agree with your content, if they feel you have sufficiently 'honourable' intent, they are a lot more likely to pay attention and engage you in discussion about it.

The Crime Of Omission

One of the communication crimes that can really ruin a reputation and mark you as having selfish intent is the crime of omission. Some people hide behind the thin veneer of deliberately leaving out information in their communications which might be important to the audience, in the hope that this puts the onus on the audience to be aware of it themselves, hoping that it provides a get-out for shifting blame if necessary. While it's not always practical or feasible to always communicate everything that should be known about any given topic, deliberate employment of this tactic is easy to spot (especially later on when situations are reviewed) and, as we shall see in the chapter on selling, is another behaviour which instantly destroys the audience's trust in the sender, making future communications and engagements so much harder as the audience is now primed to view them as a threat with selfish or ulterior motives, and likely to reject whatever communication they put out.

As we have seen from the introductory part of this chapter, when communication is halted or extremely limited, progress can slow down to a crawl, deteriorate, and sometimes go in wholly undesirable directions.

A lot of people are at a loss as to what words/pictures/music they should choose, but if you have established a clear objective and suitable intent for your communication, you will find they are a great guide in terms of both finding the right content and feeling comfortable with your final message. Of course, it helps to be aware of possible alternative meanings or different ways in which your meaning could be perceived (decoded) by your audience. Try also to get a feel as to the level of detail that your audience is going to need. If all else fails, ask them.

Chunking Up And Down

Chunking is a technique that can help us to tailor our communication on a subject to fit the needs or expectations of our audience. In effect, it is about choosing what level of detail we need to use. In written form we have to fix this to a degree, but in spoken communications we can quickly change the level of chunking if we feel that we are either providing too much detail (typical indicators may include our audience showing signs of boredom) or too little detail (they may tell us that we are stating the obvious, or ask that we expand upon the salient points). In terms of choosing the level at which to begin, experience, as well as understanding who your audience are and what they need, will aid you; but as a general rule, for business purposes I tend to begin with a high level of chunking (relatively low detail, headlines up front) to capture attention first, leaving myself with the option of delving into specific areas of audience interest later if required. To get an idea of what level of detail (or how big chunks) you may want to use, here is a summary of chunking dynamics.

Chunking Down

Providing more detail. The more detail we have, the more chance that we can see differences, and the more chance there is that something won't be quite as the audience anticipates, if they have any expectations. Chunking down can be important when examining the validity of figures, or testing whether something is true, or correct.

Chunking Up

Providing low levels of detail and more general information. Good for when you want to communicate a general picture. Because it requires less detail, there is a higher chance that you can find similarities or gain agreement at this level. In essence, chunking up is about communicating in more abstract terms about groups of ideas that can encompass wider amounts of information in simple groupings.

I once had a manager give me some pointers on this after an internal presentation. It was a short update for our team, and the schedule was pretty tight. He knew how much I loved to convey a lot of detail about any topic on which I was speaking, in the belief that I was helping my audience to learn more about it. The 15-minute slot I had was simply to make them aware of an initiative and summarise our progress. He used the following metaphor:

> *"Steve, sometimes I just want to know the time, I don't need to know how the clock works."*

This conveyed to me all I required to fit my update into those 15 minutes. For this, conveying the most important information required me to focus only very briefly on what we were doing, even less on how, with the rest devoted to why and the result. Believe me, at the start of your presenting career 15 minutes seems like a lifetime to fill. After you gain some experience, you realise it is not that long at all. Understanding whether you need to provide a higher or lower level of detail will depend entirely on your context: what effect you are trying to elicit, how this fits into the goals and viewpoint of the audience, but you now have a good view of the different directions in which you may want to head.

In terms of reviewing whether or not your message is suitable, you could go a lot further wrong than applying a simple message-building checklist constituting consideration of the following 4 Cs:

- Is it **Clear** enough?

- Is it **Concise** enough?

- Is it **Contextually** relevant to your audience?

- Do you require **Confirmation** of its reception by your audience, or their understanding of it and willingness to act upon any calls to action?

Listen Very Carefully...

With so many variables in terms of building our messages and deciding how to convey them to our audiences, perhaps one of the most important elements of communication and yet the one so frequently ignored is the ability to listen. I don't mean the ability to just notice what someone is saying. That's not listening, it's just hearing. Real listening involves seeking to understand incoming communications using whatever cues, clues and methods we have available. It requires contextual interpretation and, more often than not, confirmation with the sender that we have correctly understood the intention and meaning behind the communication to a sufficient degree. And to do that, we need to give the sender our full attention. This is what makes true listening different from merely hearing.

To be a more effective listener, approach communications you receive with an open, objective mindset. Allow the speaker to feel comfortable and safe expressing themselves, and give them your focused attention. It helps to stop talking yourself; after all, we have two ears and one mouth – a good clue that perhaps we should listen more than we talk. Look for the bigger picture if necessary – don't only focus on the content, but wonder v other things about the communication are telling you. Don't be ask questions to clarify, enhance and confirm your understar saw earlier, not asking them is the path towards stagnatior filling in knowledge gaps with our own stories and ir may or may not be correct. When people genuinely listen to one another, conversations flow easily, relationships flourish and progress is made.

DUTY OF CARE

From the proliferation of options that we and our audiences have to communicate and recommunicate quickly with a wide number of people across the globe, we can see that communication is anything but a one-directional affair. It goes out from sender to recipient, and especially in the online world of social media there is usually the opportunity for it to carry on elsewhere in hundreds, if not thousands of new directions. Sometimes we can see evidence that our message was at least received by our intended audience, for example if we can see when they retweet it, Like it or pass comment. But outside of social media, for instance when communicating with work colleagues or partners, this visibility is not usually apparent.

Sometimes, especially when working on projects, there are subsequent decisions or activities which depend on the audience's reception and understanding of the communication. In these instances, you should apply good practice and follow up with them rather than assume that this has happened. This will save you a lot of heartache and panic that can otherwise arise if you assume your audience have received, understood and acted upon a request, only to find that they assumed you would have followed it up if had been important, and as a result nothing has been done but you are now much closer to a deadline. Own your communications and take responsibility for ensuring your audience have received and understood them, and your stock as an effective communicator (and achiever) will rise.

Assuming is lazy and provides too much of an excuse for others not to do anything, and too much opportunity for everyone to try and lay the blame at someone else's door. Typical manifestations of this include statements that they either didn't notice or missed it, (accidental and easily happens when using email), didn't realise you wanted them to do something (possibly you didn't make the request for action clear or poor attention on their part but a get-out nevertheless) or didn't understand what you were asking for (in which case it would have been nice if they had come back to you to get

In terms of reviewing whether or not your message is suitable, you could go a lot further wrong than applying a simple message-building checklist constituting consideration of the following 4 Cs:

- Is it **Clear** enough?

- Is it **Concise** enough?

- Is it **Contextually** relevant to your audience?

- Do you require **Confirmation** of its reception by your audience, or their understanding of it and willingness to act upon any calls to action?

Listen Very Carefully...

With so many variables in terms of building our messages and deciding how to convey them to our audiences, perhaps one of the most important elements of communication and yet the one so frequently ignored is the ability to listen. I don't mean the ability to just notice what someone is saying. That's not listening, it's just hearing. Real listening involves seeking to understand incoming communications using whatever cues, clues and methods we have available. It requires contextual interpretation and, more often than not, confirmation with the sender that we have correctly understood the intention and meaning behind the communication to a sufficient degree. And to do that, we need to give the sender our full attention. This is what makes true listening different from merely hearing.

To be a more effective listener, approach communications you receive with an open, objective mindset. Allow the speaker to feel comfortable and safe expressing themselves, and give them your focused attention. It helps to stop talking yourself; after all, we have two ears and one mouth – a good clue that perhaps we should listen more than we talk. Look for the bigger picture if necessary – don't only focus on the content, but wonder what other things about the communication are telling you. Don't be afraid to ask questions to clarify, enhance and confirm your understanding; as we saw earlier, not asking them is the path towards stagnation and ignorance, filling in knowledge gaps with our own stories and interpretations which clarification but still, all too easily accepted as an 'accidental' reason for no action).

Avoid assuming that somebody will do it and you will help both yourself and your audience avoid these uncomfortable potential 'blame' situations. Similarly, do not be afraid to confirm to others (or seek clarification) that you have received, understood or acted upon (or intend to act upon) a request from them. Trust me, they will appreciate it.

SUMMARY

- Communication is vital to our progress; lack of it is a real threat.
- Effective communication comes from understanding it's not just about you; understand your audience too.
- Different formats have their own strengths and weaknesses and each are suited to different situations.
- Be prepared to change format if necessary.
- Don't be afraid to reach out and make your communication more personal if it will help.
- Be aware that not communicating something can be as damaging as communicating the wrong thing; contextual omission it is not a convenient excuse.
- Different levels of detail can have different effects on the audience.
- Listening is perhaps the most important of our communication tools. Be sure to make full use of it.
- Displaying a duty of care in your communications will reap rewar and save you much pain and effort.

CHAPTER 3
RELATIONSHIPS

Relationships play a huge role in modern society, and in getting things done. They are the connections that allow us to build civilisations, and to have friends and social groups. They enable us to share our differing strengths and to cover or compensate mutually for one another's weaknesses. And in doing do, they make it possible for us to do business with and work with one another to produce incredible feats that would be beyond the capabilities of any individual. The first lesson in this chapter is that if you want to have a successful career, you will need successful relationships. This is true of every single person who has made it big, no matter how that is qualified. Richard Branson. Bill Gates. Oprah Winfrey. Nobody does it alone.

A STAGGERINGLY DYNAMIC EVOLUTION

The global trend towards integration is allowing more people to meet and build relationships with one another more quickly than ever before. While not all of these relationships will be as deep as in the past, there are certainly more of them to manage thanks to several factors.

Developments In Communication

The affordability and user-friendliness of mobile phone technology has made them near-ubiquitous across most of the world, even in places where other modern conveniences are not yet as common. Social media platforms such as Facebook, LinkedIn and Twitter have connected us to a wider range of people than ever before. The ease with which we can communicate in a near instantaneous manner has enabled us to find many others who share interest in similar topics to us, leading to the creation of virtual communities and sharing of ideas and on a scale that would have been unimaginable to our grandparents when they were young.

Personal Mobility

The ease with which we can now travel to new places and meet up with people has helped make it easier to deepen whichever relationships we choose to. Travel also exposes us to many more people than in the past, many of whom go on to become new colleagues, business contacts or friends, opening up multiple new opportunities on a scale that we have never had before. It also opens up our minds to new cultures and ways of doing things – exposing us to variety and the fact that our way is not the only way.

The Speed Of Change In The World Around Us

Advances in our ability to communicate, connect and collaborate more rapidly and more easily than ever are themselves accelerating the pace of the change we effect upon the world around us. This rate of change is getting ever faster.

From a technological point of view, in 1975 Gordon E. Moore, co-founder of Intel, observed that the number of transistors that could be fitted into a dense integrated circuit would double approximately every two years. This was a revision of his first observation in 1965 that this phenomenon would occur approximately once per year, and came to be called Moore's Law.[16] While it is envisaged that this cycle will eventually reach its limit when transistors can be produced that are as small as atomic particles, it is still a generally accepted rule within the IT industry today, and ably demonstrates the exponential speed of technological progress and in the context of communication advances over the last several decades, the quite staggering cumulative impact that such a growth rate can have on economic productivity and social change.

To put the exponential growth in computing power into perspective, we can consider the ancient Indian legend of a local king who had a penchant for challenging wise visitors to his court to a game of chess. One day, he challenged a travelling sage and generously asked him to name his own prize should he win. The sage merely asked for a few grains of rice, only enough to fill a chessboard in the following manner: one grain of rice in the first square, two grains in the second, four in the third square and so on, until all of the 64 squares had been filled. The king lost the game and true to his word, honoured the sage's request by ordering a bag of rice to be brought to the table. However, he ran out of rice after only a couple of rows had been filled and quickly realised that even to get to square 20 he would need another million grains. To get to square 64 he would need several hundred billion tons of rice, or a rice mountain the size of Mount Everest. According to the legend, the sage revealed himself to be the god Krishna who agreed that the debt could be repaid over time by serving pilgrims to the king's temple a rice-based dish called paal payasam, for free, a tradition that lives on to this day in parts of India.

Regardless of the tradition it gave rise to, the story illustrates the incredible power of exponentialism. Now imagine the effect that this growth in computing power is having on our world, the incredible advances in communications and access to information it is making possible, and the changes this is making and will continue to make in shaping our relationships.

Think Quality Not Just Quantity

It may therefore be tempting to think that relationships are, as a result, rapidly becoming devalued due to the sheer number of new ones we can go out and find at the drop of a hat (we don't even need to go outside of the office to make new contacts these days). From a business point of view, that is a very limiting mindset.

Due to the also exponentially growing web of global communications and connections, what we are actually finding is that fallout from ruined relationships (especially of a business nature) is now able to spread a lot more quickly and easily than ever before. So it makes sense to ensure that we build and maintain good relationships where expectations are managed and met, reducing the amount of negative and increasing the amount of positive comment about us that is shared around the world and increasing the chances of people wanting to work with us in the future. As with the mantra extolled about customers in countless business books and methodologies, it takes a whole lot less effort to maintain good relationships with existing customers than it does to find and build new ones.

But, thanks to technology and our natural drive as a species to communicate with one another, we're still potentially gaining lots and lots of new relationships. How can we possibly have enough time to develop them all? The answer is that we can't. But not all of them require lots of time and effort to maintain to the level that our contacts are expecting. Often, it may be enough to remain on 'passing hello' terms with the majority of our contacts – keeping them as acquaintances and that's OK. But for some relationships, you need to ensure that you focus your efforts and develop much deeper, stronger understandings.

Know which of your relationships are important to you and spend time and effort developing them; more often than not, you will reap substantial rewards and interesting new opportunities out of the credibility that grows when they sing your praises to others. With the rest, you should still aim to maintain good relations, and it's simpler than you think. Much more occasional engagement can still mark you out as someone that may be worth doing business with (if and when the time should arise), as long as you remember to be consistently respectful to them as human beings.

In the film *Roadhouse*,[17] the lead character, Dalton, a renowned bouncer (referred to in the film as a 'cooler') shares with his new security team his secret to running a bar that allows clients to achieve their ends (i.e. feel good about going there to have a good time). Respect for people, even in the face of emotional volatility. If someone is acting inappropriately, ask them to leave. Nicely. If someone refuses to leave, show them to the door. Nicely. In fact, be nice at every stage until it's time not to be nice. In the film, Dalton acts as kind of executive director who has the experience to make the decision as to when the time in question has arrived (in this case, it's when the clients attack the staff). At that point he uses his experience to assist his team, but until then, the general directive of being nice to customers and treating them as human beings stands in order to help to resolve most compromising situations before they ever escalate to an extreme. As most of us aren't working in environments where the possibility of physical attack is a regular factor, there's no reason this principle shouldn't be an even more effective and achievable mantra for you to adopt regarding your work colleagues. Treat others with respect and you will see the results of their increased trust, faith and respect for you, leading to an effective workplace that benefits everyone, including the reason you are all there – your clients.

RECIPROCITY & THE GOLDEN RULE

There is a principle that has been referred to in almost every ethical community around the world throughout time, and is now typically known as the Golden Rule. The Golden Rule simply states that for a happier, more satisfying life we should treat others as we would wish to be treated ourselves. Essentially it is a very simple piece of advice that allows us to increase the opportunities available to us in life by invoking what's referred to as the ethic of reciprocity. Simply put, social psychology studies have found that if you do something nice for a person, it generates a compelling urge in them to do something nice for you in return. And vice versa, if someone does something nice for you. If fact, the size or amount of payback often outweighs the original deed offered. This is a very powerful principle to understand for work and business, and recognising it can go a long way towards helping you to build solid, sustainable relationships.

"Our prime purpose in this life is to help others. And if you can't help them, at least don't hurt them."

Tenzin Gyatzo, 14th Dalai Lama[18]

Not everyone will agree with the above statement, perhaps fewer with the first sentence, and in the context of this chapter so far, it might appear that I am suggesting that this is merely a good tactic for reasons of selfishness or personal gain. But in reality, this is advice that benefits us all for the long term. Using this principle, we each have the ability to generate reciprocated generosity by taking the initiative to offer our own time, effort or attention to others. When this is done on a repeated basis, it can create the opposite of a vicious circle – a virtuous circle, in which people forget about keeping score but get into the habit of offering support or help to one another as being a completely natural, logical and normal way of operating.

Used in light of the Golden Rule, we can see how treating people with respect, being polite to them and voluntarily offering to help them can generate respect for you both in terms of your capabilities and your intent, making it far more likely that you will have positive interactions with that person in the future. Furthermore, if you are practising this behaviour consistently (and not just being polite to a few select people) you will find that your reputation will spread throughout your organisation and often beyond, and people will enjoy and in some cases actively seek out the chance to be able to work with you. Building a good reputation for being both capable and trustworthy can open all sorts of new opportunities in the workplace; people begin to trust you with more tasks and responsibilities which often lead to more learning, recognition and experience on your part. And as your value to the organisation rises, it can also cut you some slack with your peers and managers in the event that you do make mistakes.

Many online companies have realised the principle of reciprocity and operate a business model whereby they provide free material in advance of any potential purchase, helping to achieve the two aims of giving the customer a taste of the value they stand to gain from making a purchase (establishing their credibility) and in having given some value for free, generating an urge on the part of the customer to reciprocate (ideally with a purchase). The law of reciprocity is frequently used with key customers whom an organisation has identified as being particularly desirable to keep. Sometimes better terms, freebies or perks are offered to such customers, and sometimes they are offered as additional value to try to make up for a mistake that has been made. In these situations, such activity is referred to as building goodwill.

A Note On Goodwill – What It Really Means

I feel the need to make sure you understand and use the term goodwill correctly, or it can drastically sour a relationship. Goodwill is often used to describe something that is done in addition to the expected offering to make a customer happy again when things have not turned out as expected. It is typically done entirely at the discretion of the provider, and the extra deliverable should typically be something above and beyond what the customer would have been expecting (the clue is in the words 'extra deliverable').

It should never be used to describe any result that the customer would have originally expected as part of the service, regardless of whatever trials or challenges the supplier may have had to contend with in doing so. Granted, if the customer finds out about a particularly heroic effort by the supplier to deliver the promised goods, they may well show their appreciation of the effort. But as a supplier, never try to suggest that such effort was made out of goodwill, as this implies if you hadn't been feeling particularly generous then you wouldn't have bothered (and therefore that the customer isn't important – lucky for them you were in a generous mood, hey?).

For example, in a situation where a customer was expecting free delivery but for some reason this did not happen (they were charged or the delivery simply did not occur on time), then expending the minimum effort to put the situation right (crediting the customer for the incorrect charge, or sending the product via express delivery to arrive on time) does not constitute goodwill as there has been no additional service or offering above that originally agreed. I have encountered on several occasions suppliers who have added this phrase into their explanation of what they were going to do to fix the problem to a minimally acceptable degree. Let's say that it didn't particularly endear them to me or to my future business relationship with them.

Aside from any legal consequences of not delivering the service specified, to suggest in any way that the basic making good of a bad situation the supplier has caused is in any way a bonus gift to the customer is simply an insult to their intelligence.

WORKING RELATIONSHIPS – WHERE TO FOCUS?

As mentioned earlier, we have a lot of new relationships and a limited amount of time and resource to develop them, so we have to be mindful of which ones we choose. From my experience, there are three broad types of relationship you should aim to develop and maintain well, as they are likely to be the most frequently encountered, and critical to your progress at work on a daily basis. To understand how to develop meaningful relationships with each, we will seek to understand the challenges they regularly face and how we can be a part of helping them overcome those challenges.

Key Relationship: Your Direct Manager

This person's job is to oversee the work of other people – in this case you, and possibly others. If they are at all good at their job, they will want you to do as well as you can as that makes them look good; your part of the organisation works well, supports the organisation achieving its goals and everybody wins. They can do this by:

- Ensuring you know what you are supposed to be doing, plus any specific ways in which that has to happen.

- Ensuring you are able to achieve your objectives, in terms of resources, tools, support and skills that you will need. If you are lacking in any of these, they should be discussing ways in which that lack can be overcome – whether that be securing the relevant resources, or helping you to develop your skills or approaching a particular challenge in a different way.

- Helping you to remove or overcome any other challenges that you may believe are present.

A very good manager will also be sure that you understand why it is important that you achieve your objectives (i.e. how they contribute to the overall organisational strategy) as this will often provide the motivation and drive you need to keep at the job until the goal is attained.

If you have any concerns regarding the points above, you should let your manager know as without this feedback they may not know that there is a problem, but will still be expecting you to deliver as per the expectations of your role. While they cannot always totally fix a problem situation (e.g. there just may not be any more budget or resource available), they can often come up with alternative ways to manage the situation.

Now, bear in mind that they are juggling your challenges, as well as their own, and may be doing so for many more people, so their time is going to be pretty stretched. This is why giving them good visibility on your progress can help them to be more effective in supporting you. You are essentially a team. Typically, they will organise and take care of higher, wider and larger matters so that you can concentrate on carrying out your specific activities. And being a team, as with any relationship, good proactive two-way communication is a must.

Open, Proactive Communication

Being open, proactive and concise in your communications with your direct manager will accomplish a number of things. It will make your communications more effective, and allowing them to see any challenges you face also allows them to help you with them. Being concise in your explanations means they can focus quickly on the core aspects of any issues you have rather than spending time and effort trying to digest, filter and draw understanding from a mass of both relevant and irrelevant information (while struggling to maintain the motivation to remain interested). If in doubt, err on the side of slightly over-informing; you can always dial it back a bit, but at least all of the relevant information will be on the table.

You may be able to deal with many issues on your own (in fact your manager is probably hoping you can with most), but hiding any ongoing problems under the carpet is a recipe for disaster. Firstly, the chances are that you will be found out somewhere along the way. Lies have a habit of coming back to bite people on the backside – and they tend to bite hard, as it will probably ruin your relationship with your manager as any trust that you had built up will be severely tested if not destroyed. This mistrust may spread to other parts of the organisation, adversely affecting opportunities that might have come your way if you had been regarded as trustworthy and capable. It helps to remember that context has just as important a role to play as information you willingly share. A crime of omission can lead to poor decision making just as much as poor information in the first place; as we saw in the chapter on communication, this is why it is such an anathema to work colleagues.

Being proactive and open with your manager also helps them to be better able to protect you from adverse reaction from more senior management if there is a serious problem, as they have more time to figure out ways to lay down what is sometimes described as 'covering fire' – ways of focusing senior management attention on other things allowing you to complete or deal with tricky challenges without further pressure or interference. But to be able to do this, they need to be able to understand the full picture and not just convenient details that support your story. If they support you and you string them along, sooner or later when the truth comes out you will have a whole heap of new problems, not least of which will be a manager who cannot trust you, and whom you have just made a fool of in front of other members of the organisation. Nothing suggests incompetence more than someone who doesn't know what's going on in their own area of responsibility (which in your manager's case is you), so giving them advance visibility even of issues you feel may become a difficult problem going forward also gives them time to prepare how you can both handle the situation, and will not leave them exposed as a result of your actions.

As we saw with the Golden Rule, it's all about mutual success breeding reciprocated gratitude, so helping them to look good by achieving results and keeping them up-to-date on the status of what you're working on goes a long way towards building favourable commentary on your performance that is shared with other parts of the organisation and sometimes beyond.

Think Possible Solutions, Not Just Problems

Another way that you can build strong relationships with your direct manager and make yourself a valuable team member is the way in which you approach them when you do have an issue. Most managers employ staff who are good at a specific thing that the manager either cannot do, or no longer has the time to do. In most cases they expect their staff to be able to think for themselves and make at least some of their own decisions.

CHAPTER 3: RELATIONSHIPS

While this is not to the exclusion of any challenges that may occur for which the employee is not sufficiently skilled, experienced or authorised to take, most managers would prefer their staff to at least try and figure out some possible solutions to the more difficult challenges they face before bringing them to their manager's attention. Using their experience and wider view of what's happening, they can then help their employee to make a good decision, the process of trying to find a resolution and getting guidance on it having hopefully enhanced the employee's decision-making capabilities to some degree. But simply telling your manager about a problem you face then clamming up until they come up with a solution themselves is asking a lot of their time and mental resources and can easily generate a response of, "Tell me, what do we pay you for again?" Of course they can guide you as to what elements you should consider (if you haven't done so already) in making the decision re: how to solve the challenge, but they are relying on you to do the majority of the mental legwork in at least attempting to understand the detailed context of the situation that they simply don't have the time to investigate, and providing appropriate options that may work.

Key Relationship: External Customers

While this sounds like one of the most obvious statements in the book, I will elaborate on one of the aspects of the customer-supplier relationship that I have frequently seen forgotten, ignored or never even realised in the first place: a customer's dependency upon their supplier not just for delivery of the product or service for which they are paying, but also for information about it in terms of how and when it will arrive, or the status and progress of its delivery.

One of the most consistently frustrating aspects of being a customer is needing to know information about a product or service that may affect their future decisions, but not being able to get it. I have encountered this myself on many occasions, and been involved in managing such situations as a supplier in the middle of several logistical crises. PR and spin agencies may do their best to dress up a situation for media purposes, but time and again I have found that attention-diverting tactics simply don't suffice as a solution and the truth will eventually come out, souring the company's reputation and credibility as well as providing fertile ground for competitors to jump in and save the day. I feel that if things do go seriously wrong, then honesty can often be the best policy. Of course, that honesty had better include some kind of genuine attempt to resolve the situation to the customer's satisfaction. People can sometimes be made to feel better to some degree by comforting words, but this is usually only a short-term tactic; sincere actions and attempts to remedy the core issue are usually the best medicine.

I have seen contractors who, having to remain on-site beyond the terms of their contract waiting for the late delivery of a single item, one minute fuming at not knowing when it was due to arrive, then, having been told that the supplier was doing their best (utilising a courier) to get it to them as soon as possible, even if this was after the contract deadline, accept the situation and thank the supplier for their efforts. The critical factor here is again the annoyance of not knowing. If you know something is going to be late and by how long, then you can take steps to manage the situation and its impact. Not knowing when or even if it will ever come creates a sense of paralysis; as a customer it makes the decision on how to manage the situation that much more difficult and generates worry over whether your reaction has been excessive or not. Keeping your customers informed and aware even in challenging times holds a lot of weight both in enabling them to make decisions and manage situations, and also in being able to trust you in the future.

Key Relationship: Internal Customers (Work Colleagues)

If you are working with colleagues, then you are usually both part of various processes that require you to exchange information or rely upon one another for certain actions to be completed. The moment that someone else relies upon you to provide some kind of input for them to be able to complete their part of the process, they become in effect your internal customer. This point is often forgotten as 'me focused' thinking takes over.

What Do They Need to Succeed?

As with your manager, if you want to maintain good relationships with colleagues and have them happy to work with you again, don't just heave things over the metaphorical wall and expect them to pick up the pieces. Try to understand what they need to succeed and how you may be able to hand any due elements over to them so that they are in as good a position as possible to get straight on with their task. To do this, you may want to talk to them about the task, and about their situations: what their key goals, challenges and bugbears are.

Finding out what they regard as important can also help you to identify and build an element of 'what's in it for them' just as you would with an external customer, giving them more solid reasons that are relevant to why they should want to work with you.

Removing Potential Threat

There will be times when you encounter resistance to requests for support or to proposed ideas; this sometimes happens when your colleagues either don't fully understand what is required, why it is important, or they question why they should believe you (i.e. question your credibility).

Providing them with clear guidance and context can resolve the first two, but the last of these may be caused by them being anxious at following a newcomer; lack of credibility is not an uncommon situation for a person new to a team to find themselves in. Without any information about you, your potential threat level is high by default on at least two counts; your colleagues' inner chimpanzees may seek to protect them from unidentified potential danger by imagining the worst case scenario causing them to either doubt your capability or your intent.

To overcome the credibility gap, there is no faster way than demonstrating results, ideally being able to do so on this job with some quick wins that you can all benefit from. However, before we can do this, it can pay to address the intent element in order to help buy you time to be allowed to demonstrate your capabilities. People are more open to someone they know a little about, so it pays to forge some kind of social bond with your colleagues early on. Being willing to participate in non-work-related conversation is a good way that requires little more in the way of situational set-up than a simple cup of coffee or a few moments away from the formality of your desks. Especially when working with people for the first time, a little ice-breaking at the beginning can make everyone more comfortable as you learn a little more about each other – assuming everyone has the right intent and are not displaying any other signs that indicate they should be treated with suspicion.

Key Relationship: External Partners

Though many people regard external suppliers as merely faceless commodities – one of many who would jump at the chance of getting their business – it can pay to view them as partners with whom a long-term mutually beneficial relationship should be sought. Sustainable relationships can mean your supplying partners gaining a better understanding of your needs as a customer and you will spend less time explaining these to new suppliers who may or may not get them anyway. Again, working effectively with external partners requires mutual integrity. If you respect the fact that they are human beings with their own business concerns who are also trying to make a living and treat them accordingly, such as paying them on time, and being polite, you will enjoy much easier, more rewarding supplier relationships. By communicating as clearly and honestly as you can, you will avoid costly misunderstandings that can cause someone to lose out, creating tension that sours relationships. You will also foster genuine goodwill that helps to smooth out informally many minor issues that may crop up.

CRITICAL CONVERSATIONS

There will be times when you need to have difficult conversations with colleagues about problems such as poor performance or unmet expectations. These kinds of conversations can be especially difficult when there is a lot at stake, and as a result emotions have the potential to run high. So how can you do this without burning the bridges of any relationships you may have with them; surely if your winning means they lose, then it's an open and shut case that someone will finish up unhappy? As we have seen in our relationship with our direct manager, it pays to be open and not to hide or dilute our message. This is not to say that you should charge in like a bull in a china shop. But as we saw with the *Roadhouse* cooler, we should seek to pursue our objective (resolve the problem) while having respect for the feelings and rights of others as human beings, people with their own challenges, perceptions and contexts.

So how can we do that? There are a number of steps we can take to help us get there; it pays to take a look at yourself first. Be honest about your objective: is it simply 'to win', or attain a goal that you can both agree is acceptable? Be prepared to explain objectively why you believe something has to happen, and the consequences of it not happening. Doing this can help you to see if a more open-minded approach might be useful in order to consider alternative options and, if required, help you to adjust your outlook. Zoom out from the detail and look at the longer term consequences or bigger picture if necessary. If you can find a level at which you can both agree on a shared pool of meaning (i.e. an outcome related to the issue that you both agree should be the driving goal), then it is easier to lay out objectively any sticking points you each see about getting there, and be able to work together to find a workable solution.

Not finding a common goal to head towards keeps us each confined within our own small circle of need, uncomfortable in sharing objectively and maintaining our respective hidden agendas. The perceived threat coming from the belief that someone is hiding their true intent and the ensuing lack of trust this generates serves only to stoke emotional reaction further leading to defensive behaviour, stopping communication or even assigning blame.

Depersonalising the words you use and the way in which you describe the situation from your point of view can also help here – try using the passive voice. By describing exactly what is happening (almost as if you were trying to write it down as if it were a process), and sticking only to the facts that you know to be true, you can make it safer for others to feel comfortable also being open about the facts. You now know that your mind has a tendency to make up sometimes exaggeratedly scary stories to fill in information gaps and 'keep you safe', so whatever you do, don't apportion blame and just stick to the facts. This way you stand a better chance of being able to have a conversation in which both of you feel safe enough to address the issue in an open, objective and honest way.

If at any point you feel that people are reacting defensively or aggressively, then chances are they do not feel safe enough. As long as your intent is honourable, leaving the topic of the content for a moment to outline the mutual objective of the conversation (the shared meaning or goal) can help to get things back on track, or at least give you both the chance to discuss why you feel unsafe and what could be done about it.

I once faced such a situation where I had to ask a colleague (a more senior manager in a separate department) to make an engineering change to a part specification document for some product labels. The second time I went back to ask him for another change, he became rather annoyed at what he regarded as continual interruptions to his (main) work. Sensing his mood, I outlined my objective, why this was important for the company, and acknowledged his frustration. I also shared the fact that being new (my first couple of months in my first job in fact) I was at a loss to find a way to attain my goal without his help. We soon came to the conclusion that a mutually acceptable solution could include me being able to make required changes to the label's engineering specifications without the need for him to be involved. After approving this with my manager, he was then able to show me how to do it correctly, and we had in fact found a solution by re-engineering the specification document amendment process.

Focusing on the process and not the person makes it easier to talk openly about what is happening as people feel less threatened – you are analysing the results of a process rather than questioning their abilities. Conversation then tends to flow more freely and creatively, mutually acceptable solutions are more likely to be found with little or no detrimental effect on the relationship. Of course, in order for people to want to engage in this kind of mutual issue-solving conversation with you, they need to feel comfortable enough to share their exact feelings and thoughts – and for that to happen there is a big factor that needs to be present: trust!

Trust

If there is no trust or even low levels of trust, then progress is extremely difficult. Decisions are made for the wrong reasons – often selfish ones (i.e. to protect individual interests or to deal with what are perceived as potential personal threats), at the expense of the optimum decision for the company or other stakeholders involved. Progress slows or can be halted dead in its tracks, and even when people do decide to work with one another, they may feel the need to put safety mechanisms into the process in order to protect themselves, leading to slower, more complicated, more costly processes. And at work, time is money!

Author Stephen M. R. Covey[19] sums this up with a simple formula that states the more trust there is in a relationship, the faster processes can flow and the less costly it is to conduct them. Looking at the key elements of trust, one can see that there are several different kinds of trust, some of which we have already touched on.

Trust in a person's capabilities. Do they have the skills to perform what is being asked of them?

Trust in a person's integrity – will they keep their promises?

Trust in a person's intent – are they doing this solely for the purposes of their own advancement, or is there also some kind of benefit for me that they genuinely want to help me gain – mutual benefit?

Covey also extolls a fourth type of trust – trust in the results that you deliver. It has to be said that development of trust does not rely on delivering results alone, or any single one of the other elements for that matter. I have met and worked with people who frequently delivered results but whose methods could be described as Machiavellian. In one instance, very few, if any people that I knew in the company trusted them, which meant that getting those results was usually very costly for the company, both in terms of getting to the result and the unseen cost of the fallout that getting there in that way created. However, results can be one of the clearest and fastest ways to prove you are capable and driven enough to deliver on your promises, and if you can do that in an ethical, respectful way that leaves people happy to work with you again, then you will find that your colleagues and customers quickly pick up on your honourable intent. They will support your future efforts more readily, progress is a lot more easily achieved, and challenges can be quickly overcome even in situations where difficult or sensitive conversations need to be undertaken – because people feel safe in being open with the facts, allowing for genuine exploration of the issue.

Ownership & Accountability

One way of getting results and building trust is to be proactive. As is taught to children the world over, being sorry is not simply about saying the words, it's about doing something to show you mean them. Trust is simply a by-product of people who take actions which demonstrate their intent, integrity or capability. Volunteer for work or new projects if you have the capacity. Take ownership of something that needs somebody to drive or own it to make it work, or work better. At the very least, take ownership for driving your own career and progress; in most cases, this should lead to you owning things that support your goal and being able to get results and build trust.

On the one hand, yes, you could lumber yourself with lots of extra work. But it's far more likely that you'll earn a lot of respect for both your abilities and especially your attitude. And very often in these situations, all it takes to succeed is a little desire and effort put into organising things. Having a proactive attitude and taking ownership of completion of a task or project is in fact a vital leadership skill that will help you to get recognised and stand you in good stead for future career moves. Even if you aren't looking to climb the career ladder and are happy where you are, it will build you a rock solid reputation for getting things done (hopefully in the right way), and in the modern workplace such credibility is one of the most valuable staff assets which money alone can't always buy.

Leadership and the right attitude are often the missing ingredients that organisations crave, and the most sought after qualities in the recruitment process. If you can build a reputation as someone who gets things done the right way and doesn't let them slide, people will come to you asking for support or even advice, and though it won't necessarily make you into a leader from a reporting point of view, having people working for you is not the goal of true leadership. Helping ensure that your actions support and give the best chance of success to your colleagues and organisation is, and can be a big factor in giving you opportunities and the chance to choose your future path for yourself.

SUMMARY

- Technology is giving us easier access to more relationships, but remember to develop some more deeply.

- Applying the Golden Rule will generate you a lot of social capital and save you much effort and grief.

- Managers prefer not to be surprised and will appreciate attempts to help them help you long before things develop into an emergency.

- Internal customers appreciate collaborative efforts to hand issues over rather than have the issues land on them.

- Difficult conversations over important issues require objectivity, a shared goal and openness to resolve them; for this, trust is vital.

- Attitude can be a critical differentiator that marks you out as a valuable employee; be prepared to take ownership of and be accountable for making things happen.

CHAPTER 4
MAKING DECISIONS

One of the most useful skills for making progress at work is the ability to make decisions. We can consider a decision as being a trigger for action to begin. Before we can take action, we have to decide to take some action, and if so, which action to take.

It sounds pretty straightforward, and it can be, although the emphasis on choosing correctly that both we and the world at large now place on making good decisions is leading to them getting harder and harder to make. Or at least, we perceive that it is getting harder to make the right decision. Beware of this kind of polarised 'sucker's choice' thinking where we believe there only to be a limited number of options, typically 'right' or 'wrong', 'this option' or 'that one'. It is so easy to become so fixated on making the absolutely perfectly optimised decision, searching for the mythical 'right' decision (even though we don't necessarily even know what that would look like), that we are spending ever more time trying to make sure we have done just that. And it's not as if the number of options we face on any given aspect of our working day is getting any smaller.

TOO MUCH CHOICE?

With practically anything you look at these days – supplier choice, product variant, analysis method, software tools – we are faced with so many variables that it becomes incredibly difficult for us to be sure that we are making the best choice. And yet we still believe that it is possible. In his book *The Paradox of Choice* which goes into detail on this phenomenon, psychologist Barry Schwartz describes the mind-boggling number of options available to him when simply trying to pick a salad dressing at his local supermarket. And in terms of the number of possible different options he has when building a home audio system, he calculates that he could feasibly construct over six million different system variants using the components in his local hi-fi store.[20]

This avalanche of choice that has been generated by the free, untethered boom of capitalism, while generally a better scenario than having little or no choice at all, falls foul of the law of unintended consequences. In wanting to make the absolute best choice that you can, there is a danger that you can succumb to paralysis by analysis – delaying or not making a choice because you simply cannot decide which combination of decisions and choices would give you the optimum result. This is a typical symptom of people adopting what Schwartz describes as a 'Maximiser' approach. By investing copious amounts of time and effort researching and, if necessary, testing all of the options available, Maximisers hope to reach that optimum result. But if it leads to us making the right decision each time, then isn't this a good thing? If time itself were not an issue, perhaps. But we are time-bound, we only have a finite amount of time on this earth as living creatures; moreover, at work we often have limited periods of time that we can reasonably spend on any one thing before we have to make some kind of decision or take some kind of action.

Think about the hi-fi store. Not many of us have infinite amounts of time or resource to try out and test every one of the vast number of possible combinations. So in this instance, considering the growing number of choices presented to us coupled with the limitations on our capacity to explore them all, it's almost guaranteed from the start that we are not going to get that perfect result. Secondly, who says it's the best choice or decision?

How can you be sure? Unless you are taking part in a competition with highly defined and commonly accepted rules such as a sporting event, it's almost impossible to know what is the best decision, as everyone will have different opinions on what is important.

DEFINE YOUR CRITERIA FOR SUCCESS

To remedy this, we could define what success should look like – or in the case of decisions, what factors are important, upon what criteria should our decisions be based? We could use our own experience, or take our definitions from the guidance of others. Basing decisions on whether or not they support the organisation's strategy is a fairly sound approach, while talking to others is a great way of understanding existing definitions or expectations of what success looks like that may need to be heeded, both in terms of learning from their experience and in terms of understanding what your organisation's culture is likely to accept. By asking them to share their decision-making criteria, often you can help to simplify the process by alleviating them of the decision-making effort. Of course you need to demonstrate that you are capable of evaluating well enough, but by talking to people already making these decisions and asking them why they are choosing particular courses of action, you can begin to build your map of what to do and when.

Alternatively, we could use our own intuition to figure out what might be important to our decisions. We will see more about this in the chapter on imagination later on, but suffice to say that on a simple level, we could draw up a list of factors that:

- Are absolutely essential to our decisions (must haves).

- Could have an influence if there is no difference between the available options with regard to must haves (nice to haves).

This simplification can often help us make decisions when we are unsure about why we should go for one option over another. So we have a couple of ways of building our decision-making platform by defining what properties or parameters the outcome must possess. But there's another twist.

NOTHING IS PERFECT, EVERYTHING IS RELATIVE

Deep down we know that it's almost impossible to have made the perfect choice, and knowing this leads to side effects such as dissatisfaction or even anxiety. Sometimes we pour ever more time and effort into researching and checking to be sure we have made the best choice – delaying matters. Sometimes we will procrastinate and worry about making the 'right' choice before making our decision because of this ambiguity, again leading to delayed progress and increased stress levels. And after we have made it, it is not uncommon for us to look at other options that may appear and begin to compare them to the choice we made. When we find options that we believe or imagine may have been a better choice, we then worry post-decision about what could have been and about what we lost out on: the opportunity cost, or the perceived differential in return on the resource or time invested between what we did and the other option. This can lead to buyer's remorse, or dissatisfaction with the decision that was made – and even more anxiety.

What's more, further anxiety is heaped upon us in modern society when we realise that whatever outcomes we experience, by having so much choice, then these outcomes have been largely shaped by us, not by unavoidable circumstance, and we often enter a vicious circle of self-blame, mentally beating ourselves up about it, causing us to strive harder to ensure we get it right the next time, leading to further delays and another loop of the circle leading to more self-directed negativity. On balance, with so many options, as we have established, the chances of getting it absolutely right and perfect are pretty much non-existent.

This concept of perfectionism has a lot to answer for, and it is frequently found to lie at the crux of procrastination. If we tend to avoid discomfort or failure because it represents a threat, then even though taking action might only hold the possibility of failure, believing that there is a perfect solution or outcome (which we know by its nature is unachievable) instantly guarantees to us that we will fail and sparks the avoidance reaction. By exploring its properties more, perhaps we can learn ways to deal with it. The term 'perfect' is a highly subjective one. As we have seen when looking at the multiple tools, systems and methodologies available to us, each has its strengths and weaknesses in any given context, and often it is the context which defines what is a good fit or not. Equally, what works and what doesn't work well is merely a judgment based upon both context and our interpretation, which will vary from person to person. Even when we think we have found perfection, in reality there isn't anything that can't be improved upon in some way.

WHEN GOOD ENOUGH IS GOOD ENOUGH

So, if we accept that there are no magical silver bullets, and that nothing can ever be the pinnacle of perfection, then don't we have a good reason right there why we should stop striving for it? This last statement isn't as defeatist as it sounds. It is in fact a highly effective coping mechanism, allowing us to cope with the multiple possibilities that life has to offer. By trying to maximise too much, we can develop a growing dissatisfaction with the results and our general level of happiness and satisfaction can suffer as we realise that our failure to attain perfection is, because of the choices available to us, our own fault. Sometimes it may pay to put in that extra effort, but we have seen that we should define the limits of what is important so that we can tell when we have achieved our goal to a sufficiently acceptable degree. We should be choosy about where we employ a maximising approach, evaluate the impact and return that the decision may have upon our work lives (even our lives) and invest our time and effort accordingly.

There will be some circumstances where the returns that we get are simply not worth the amount of effort it would take to make the absolute best decision, as in the hi-fi example. In those situations, we should recognise that making a decision that's good enough will more than likely help our progress to a recognisably significant degree as if we had gone a lot further in our research.

By employing this 'good enough' approach, we open ourselves to having the option of adopting a strategy that Barry Schwartz calls 'Satisficing'. Instead of piling the pressure on ourselves to always be the best, to make the perfect decisions every time, we can avoid much of the anxiety of maximising by simply striving to attain an acceptable result or level of performance. This pays off not just in allowing us to feel better about individual decisions, but also by freeing us from paralysis by analysis so that we can continuously make series of decisions that are good enough, and are able to get out of our own way.

Getting To Good Goes A Long Way

Aiming for good over perfect can have a positive effect on the way we set our objectives. Instead of trying to complete the whole objective in one go, just try for a little better: identify what would be the next small, yet nonetheless demonstrably improved level of performance and aim for that. If that sounds too easy, or unambitious, the trick is that when we complete it, we don't stop, but we look to the next level and focus on that, and keep repeating as we progress. And therein lies the way to improve performance to truly excellent levels – to stop striving for perfection, but instead to ensure that we are continuously making one step after another, each one bringing us a little closer towards it, sure in the knowledge that this is the path towards satisfaction, through continuous achievement and progress. Simply aiming for a small improvement is achievable. It can also be more easily measured so that we can judge whether or not we have made any progress, or whether our actions, driven by our choices, had any effect in making a defined situation better. The great thing about better is that there is always something else to aim for, so we never run out of goals to drive us onwards.

And it is this philosophy that underpins a highly practical method by which decision making can be made very quick and easy, leading to consistent action and continual results, feedback, learning opportunities and progress. The principle is this: when faced with a decision, ask yourself three questions:

1. Will it help us improve/make progress? (And can we easily demonstrate that?)

2. Is it legal?

3. Would I be comfortable telling someone else whose respect I value, e.g. a close relative, about this? (i.e. is it morally acceptable to do this?)

If you cannot answer yes to the first question, you may need to do more research (assuming you don't already believe the answer to be a definite no).

If you cannot answer yes to question 2, then I would recommend that you either don't make that choice, or if the answer may be subject to legal interpretation, then you will probably want to seriously weigh up the consequences of it turning out to be no.

Question 3 checks for a moral imperative. While some businesses have in the past been prepared to adopt an 'it's legal, so it's OK' stance, due to the ease and speed of modern communications, more and more we are seeing moral judgments of the population at large having a significant effect on organisational success. When British MPs were found to have been claiming expenses for the costs of what many members of the voting public regarded as frivolous luxuries, though it was within the scope of what they were legally allowed to do, many were castigated for attempting to do so in a time of austerity as it was felt that this showed contempt for the people they were supposed to be serving, and who were in fact paying their salaries and for all of the parliamentary privileges they enjoy. In essence, it wasn't congruent with existing societal expectations or zeitgeist. In another example, some global corporations have attempted to maximise their profits by taking advantage of legislation that allows them to restructure their assets or officially registered business locations to geographies which have tax laws more favourable for their business than the UK. In the UK, this is a perfectly legal practice thanks to a ruling which states that organisations are allowed to pursue any legal means of minimising their tax obligations that they wish, just as much as the government is allowed to pursue in any legal way it wishes the reclamation of any due taxes which fall within the scope of UK tax laws.

However, legal as these restructuring moves may have been, when the practice was exposed in the media, again it struck many individuals as unfair that this should be allowed to happen; the organisation enjoying the benefits of operating in the UK market at incredibly low net tax rates while many people were having to tighten their own belts, and there was a rapid escalation in the number of morally outraged potential customers of these organisations who threatened to and did boycott their products unless they took suitable action to stop and make amends.

DECIDING IS DESTINY

If a decision ticks all three boxes with a resounding yes, then you probably have a solid foundation for making the decision and moving ahead. Here's something else to bear in mind: choosing to make no decision at all is still a decision and will have consequences. Don't necessarily think that just because you have chosen not to act that the world will indefinitely stop until you are ready. Whether you make a choice from among several options or choose not to, there will always be an outcome, so rather than hiding from decisions and letting the randomness of pure chance decide, you may as well take advantage of the options and possibilities you have been lucky enough to be blessed with and at least have a chance of guiding your life in the directions you would prefer.

Focusing that power in the right direction can be accomplished by simply noticing what elements of a given situation are within your control, and which aren't. What efforts do you honestly believe you would be prepared to commit to in order to attain your desired outcome?

There are some major factors that influence our working lives such as government decisions on interest rates or foreign policy. If you're not prepared to commit to the huge amount of time and effort that is likely to be required to change this (joining opinion-forming organisations, establishing pressure groups, organising public mobilisations of protest, petitioning government departments, etc.) then it is a good bet that you can classify that as being out of your control, and may need to find another way to deal with it than prevention.

However, there are a great many factors that we *can* control in terms of what decisions we make and what actions we take. Research to identify what makes high achievers hit the heights they do compared to everyone else has consistently shown that innate talent is a rarity and that even elite level performers have achieved their success simply via consistent, proactive action. For this to happen, they needed to decide to do things. They also needed to decide *what* to do, though as many of them will testify, whether they succeeded or failed in every decision was not the issue. As we see in other chapters, most of them failed a lot, but the simple fact that they kept on making decisions and taking action based on these decisions is how they learnt what worked and made progress.

Accept Your Imperfections

To be truly comfortable with the idea of not shying away from making decisions, we must accept that in making decisions that lead to action it is inevitable that we will make some mistakes – we're not perfect either. And from a purely statistical point of view, the more decisions we take, the more mistakes we are also going to make, correct? Well yes, but looking at the bigger picture, in making decisions we stand to gain far more then we stand to lose.

As we shall see in the chapter on learning, taking action and actually doing something delivers some of the richest feedback when learning any given activity. If we do not take action simply out of apathy, this could be considered a waste of the opportunity that life has given us, and let's face it, none of us ever really know just how much of it we have left to use.

The more decisions we make, the more opportunities we have to get feedback on what worked and what didn't, the faster we can learn and the more progress we stand to make.

For most of us, it's not a one-shot deal at being the best in the world; it's simply about being better than you were before – and that is a journey which requires learning and as a result, mistakes. (Hint: the learning part is supposed to help us avoid making exactly the same mistake twice. To paraphrase Einstein, doing something the same way and expecting a different result is the definition of insanity.)

Forecasting is a great example: take any subject where people forecast – financial markets, national weather centres. Many of these have countless experts pouring hours of analysis into the mix, but still no one can predict with absolute certainty what is going to happen next. Essentially the whole concept of forecasting is about predicting the future, and because of the universe's infinite complexity and as a result, tendency to throw in completely unexpected combinations of factors (as we glimpsed with chaos theory at the start of the book), forecasting is expected to be wrong, just as nothing in the world is '100% efficient'!

Because there is no such thing as perfect, it's mainly about getting better at being less wrong – but recognising that there is always room for improvement. So stop beating yourself up about things that are less than perfect (as they never will be); celebrate the progress you did make from each decision (even if the only progress was the learning experience) and get excited about the amazing opportunity that you have to learn such a lot!

Mistakes are such a natural part of the learning curve in fact, that every single successful person has made them, plenty of them. They haven't set out to fail of course. But they have accepted that as a consequence of increasing the number of new things and ideas that they have tried and explored, they were going to get some of them wrong – at least until they had learnt how to perform that particular skill well. And in allowing themselves to try new things out, to test new ways, they quickly learnt a lot and found out how to be effective.

> *"I have constructed 3,000 different theories in connection with the electric light... only in two cases did my experiments prove the truth of my theory."*
>
> **Thomas A. Edison,
> inventor of the long-lasting filament light bulb**[21]

Yes, it is possible that some decisions could have a major negative impact on your career or be life-threatening, but remember this:

a. For most of us, the terminal ones are pretty few and far between.

b. The three checklist questions listed above should guide you safely past most of the big ones that only occasionally come along.

c. With many decisions it is simply impossible to know the long-term machinations. Many of these effects will be out of your control anyway, so it's pointless to spend too much time worrying about them. But remember this. As each decision generates new situations, there will be many, many more opportunities for you to adjust things and correct your course along the way – so accept that there will be second, third and even fourth chances and don't be afraid to utilise their potential to help you make decisions now.

As long as we take care to see that we (and others) can survive our mistakes, and take steps to ensure that we learn from each one so as to avoid repeating the same error over and over, then coming to appreciate the value that mistakes can give us goes a long way to empowering our decision making.

What if you find you're working in a place that doesn't encourage mistakes and learning? If that's the case, and it is a problem for you (or if it's a problem for the rest of us, such as one of those roles where the impact of mistakes is much higher), then it may be wise to re-evaluate your career path and plan and move to somewhere that does allow you to grow.

So for the overwhelming majority of decisions we have to make on a daily basis, our mistakes won't end our world or anyone else's. But it would be good to feel better about making them at the time, right? As well as feeling more comfortable making them, this brings us on to ways in which we can also get better at making them, even when we don't have perfect evidence.

Dealing With Ambiguity

"I'd rather we had problems because of something we did rather than something we didn't."

I have heard this repeated and paraphrased by quite a number of successful colleagues I have worked both for and with and for whom I have great respect in their abilities to get results. In essence, they are making a statement on several levels:

- Organisations pay people to do things, generally they don't pay them not to.

- In making a mistake, at least it shows that the person has been doing something in an effort to move things forward (the right staff intent and attitude are incredibly important as without them, very little indeed can happen).

- They recognise progress comes through learning what works and what doesn't – and one of the best ways to learn about something is to do it.

Most of them have also applied the principle to themselves, not just their staff and co-workers. In trying to understand how they were able to make decisions even when faced with a short window and minimal available information, I consistently received the same answer: they used what evidence they had available and made sure they had a reason for the decisions they had taken. Sometimes it may have turned out to be the wrong decision, but they knew they could always demonstrate the basis for their thinking at the time. This at least allowed them to review and identify where they needed to learn about or receive support on what they might need to do differently the next time, or to highlight areas of the decision-making process that could be improved to better enable them to make a more informed decision. In short, they could always justify their 'why', and this gave them the confidence to make decisions. I found it such a simple and yet so empowering a concept, more so when applied to situations when you need other people to make a decision that affects whether or not you can proceed. So much so that I incorporated it into countless induction talks to new starters that I have delivered over the years in companies at which I have worked. In fact, I believed giving people the skills and understanding that would help them to help others make decisions was so important that I often used it to wrap up my sessions:

"If you remember nothing else about what I have rambled on about today, please just remember Steve's Two Golden Rules Of Working Here (or anywhere for that matter):

- Rule 1: If you want someone to make a decision for you, help them to be able to justify it to their boss, and here's why. They may be asked to justify it by their boss, and their boss may have to justify it to their boss and so on up the reporting chain to the point where the chief exec asks, "Why did we decide to do that?" If they can all feel comfortable enough explaining the reasoning why, then you have a great chance of getting a favourable response.

- Golden Rule number 1 works hand in hand with Steve's Golden Rule number 2: Change your perspective of the decision maker; they most likely deal with these kinds of requests and decisions every day and thus are probably subject matter experts in this area. So, instead of seeing them as some kind of gatekeeper or obstacle that must be overcome, view them as consultants who are in an excellent position to advise you on what they or the company needs to see for everyone to feel good about going with your idea. To elicit this expertise, just ask them. Talk to them. Preferably in person or on the phone as it is more personal and will build your relationship more effectively than simply asking them to state it via email."

What we're doing here is empowering other people's decision making – and often it comes from asking the right questions that help them to help you. I experienced this principle on a regular basis in one company when I was working with key account managers who were getting angry with our new strategic pricing manager. He had quickly built up a reputation with them for being belligerent and unhelpful. Upon asking why, they told me that he was refusing to give them the discount levels they wanted for proposals they were putting together. As it was part of my job to help resolve issues like this, I had a chat with the pricing manager to find out the reasons why he was refusing to give pricing that I knew we were able to accommodate and had done on several other occasions (and also to understand the other half of the conversations between him and the account managers). He told me straight: the pricing requests he was receiving were insufficient in detail for him to justify agreeing to such discounts. There was no reason why given in the requests, and no information that pointed to why it made commercial sense, just the products, quantities and price levels. He'd sent an email to let the account managers know what he required in these requests and felt it had been ignored, so was now playing hardball using their own tactics. All he needed was some evidence or detail demonstrating a strategic imperative; beyond winning the value of this project, how else did we as a company stand to benefit? Were there larger volumes to come, had we identified further opportunities in the pipeline with the customer? Were they a significant name that could boost our credibility in a target market? Were there marketing opportunities that we could leverage, or was it vitally important that we stop a competitor from gaining a foothold in this account?

In most instances, a couple of short conversations later and the pricing manager received revised requests that he was happy to agree to. The discount level was the same, yet there were demonstrable reasons and supporting evidence as to why it was important that we do this. A few of the account managers got it straight away, and began to provide more detail in their submissions, sometimes even calling him up to discuss, in his view, what exactly would be required for him and the company to feel comfortable agreeing to them. On some occasions, despite extremely aggressive discount requests, he personally defended and drove for their approval up to vice presidential levels, because he understood (and could show) why it made sense for the company's longer term future. Of course some of the account managers continued to need the occasional reminder after having submitted particularly scanty requests. But throughout, he remained defender of the company's profits, gained a lot of respect from both key account managers and senior executive management, and sales on these key accounts grew even throughout the global recession period as he had adhered (and ensured everyone else adhered) to the principle: be able to justify, justify, justify. This principle alone can help you to free yourself and others from the bonds of indecision as it gives you the confidence to take and drive action, knowing that you and others will be able to explain why it makes sense to do so.

RISK

Other ways of bolstering your confidence can include taking some time to evaluate the risks that you may associate with choosing to follow a particular path and taking steps to manage those risks. Risk can appear quite scary, but by investigating it we can better understand its true nature and take steps to remove some of the fear of the unknown.

Risk Evaluation: A Simple Yet Effective Method

At a very basic level, relative risk can simply be ascertained in quite a simple way, and by relative, I mean a level of risk that is either acceptable to you (so you feel comfortable making a particular choice) or not (you don't make that choice). It can be viewed as the product of three primary factors:

a. What are the chances that the activity will go wrong if carried out once?

b. What would be the impact if it went wrong once?

c. How many times is the activity going to be carried out?

The higher any of the factors is, the more you need to think about how many failures (if any) you would be prepared to or be able to withstand. So for instance, if we said that performing a particular activity stands a 50% chance of going wrong, that we are going to perform it once and if it does go wrong it will cost us £500, then we could say that as long as we are prepared to hold a contingency of £500 aside at least until we have completed the activity, we are prepared to go ahead.

If, however, we are going to perform the activity 100 times, then it may be wise to hold a lot more in contingency depending on how risk averse we are (remember, risk evaluations are like forecasts – estimations based upon what we think will happen in the future). We may end up using none of it (if all operations turn out to be 100% successful) or all of it (if every attempt fails), but if we take a big precaution, we could be reasonably confident that even given the worst case scenario, we could survive. This is the principle of only risking what you can afford to lose, and while conservative in appearance, is quite a sensible approach to most risk.

Managing Risk

As we can see from the three risk dynamics outlined above, there are a number of risk mitigation strategies we could employ to deal with each. Let's take a look at activity such as crossing the road to illustrate them and how we might evaluate whether they are fit for purpose in this instance.

Strategy 1: Reducing the impact of each potential failure

Crossing the road is pretty dangerous for humans. Being hit at speed by a powerful, heavy lump of metal means that just one failure is likely to result in serious injury or even death. Perhaps we could reduce the impact somewhat by making cars out of softer material? Maybe instead (or in addition) we could wear thick bubble-wrap suits and helmets to improve the cushioning of any impacts that occur? Maybe we could reduce the speed at which cars can or are allowed to travel? While the first two are highly impractical, the third idea might work to a degree, but would take a heck of a lot of effort to pull off (certainly for us as individuals), and even with speed limits, there's still no guarantee that everyone will obey them. Let's see if a different strategy might work better.

Strategy 2: Reducing the number of times we perform the activity

Again, while we could try to avoid crossing the road (at least as frequently), at some point it is inevitable that we will have to – unless we are happy to live extremely limited lives trapped within our existing block of pavement and buildings. So in this instance, again, somewhat impractical.

Strategy 3: Reducing the chances of it going wrong each time it is performed

OK, we may be on to something here. We could do this by learning how to cross the road well – what is good practice here? We could ask someone who appears to be able to do it well to show us or explain. We could ask them to do it with us for the first few times until we feel (or maybe more objectively, until they feel) we have got a good grasp of the skill. We could reduce the chances of failure even further by making our early practice attempts on quiet roads and gradually increasing the difficulty as we get better at it. In our learning we may find that there are safer places to cross and pick up useful good practices such as the 'Stop, Look, Listen, Think' mantra, which has been promoted to children in the UK since the 1970s by the Royal Society for the Prevention of Accidents. This strategy in this context appears to offer quite a lot of scope for reducing the risk until we get to a level at which despite the still high level of potential risk from the first two factors (impact of a failure and number of times we will cross a road), we can greatly minimise the chance of it going wrong to such a degree that we can evaluate the chances of failure automatically out of habit.

So you can see, being able to evaluate quickly these three aspects of risk can really help us to build ways that make us feel more comfortable taking them – if that is needed to make progress.

Beware Of Bias

When evaluating risk, or return for that matter, it is important to know your data – and due to emotional stimulus, we're not always the best at making good judgments in this regard. We can easily be swayed by factors that cause an emotional reaction, whether pleasant or otherwise. An example? Using traffic again, you are far more likely to die from crossing the road in a traffic accident than you are from air travel – and yet a lot more people have a significant fear of flying than do crossing the road or driving. This is more than likely due to gaps in our understanding of the principles of avionics and the rigorous attention and standards that are applied to air travel, plus the information that we do have readily to hand. Media coverage of the relatively few air crashes that happen each year tends to focus on the result of the impact, which in most cases tends to be fatal. No wonder our lizard brains cling on to this clear and present threat and set our emotional alarm bells ringing more easily than when we are just running across the road in the same old way that we have done all of our lives and lived to experience over again countless times more without really even thinking about it. Again, we can see the influence that familiarity has over even potential life or death situations.

Another factor that skews our ability to evaluate effectively is confirmation bias. Our minds are built to find meaning in things, even when there is none. This is how we are able to look at clouds or patterns in a carpet and find faces or recognisable images of other things within those patterns. We are looking for things and so we filter and shape the incoming stimuli we receive to find them. These are examples of randomly finding random meaning in random things – cases in which we usually do not know what we will find until we are exposed to the stimulus (the clouds, the wallpaper patterns) and our minds have a chance to play with it and figure out what we know that it reminds us of. But if we are searching for reasoning to reinforce a specific belief, then this innate drive to mould our perception into something meaningful can be especially potent at shaping whatever we experience to fit the meaning that we expect to find. If we are thinking of buying a green car, we begin to notice more green cars around us and start to believe that there are a strangely inordinate number of green cars on the road, when in fact they were there all along, we just didn't notice them as we weren't previously primed to notice them. If we believe there is an agenda against our football team, we tend to focus on the 'evidence' that 'proves' our belief, often to the exclusion of other data that if considered, makes our supporting evidence seem much less of a clear case and more like the random variation in circumstance that it probably is. And so when we evaluate what we are being shown, or seek to illustrate a fact using data at work, we should take a moment to check whether or not there is more that we should consider. This can reduce the chances of us succumbing to this highly subjective yet all too human trait of seeing only what we want or expect to see.

Understand Your Data

When evaluating data, we should also seek to understand it in terms of its validity. We can do so in a number of ways, including understanding more about its source – is it independent and credible, are there any clues that could reveal its true nature in the context of the situation, and what are they really telling you?

We've already mentioned how adjectives such as 'the best' can be highly subjective terms. In what exact capacity is it the best? How can we be sure of that? And relatively speaking, what difference does that make, why is that important? (The 'so what?' test.)

The same applies to claims such as 'faster' – than what? Or 'new and improved'– in what way? Percentages are a classic example of the relativity of data, and how it can be presented to sound great initially with a high figure, but once examined in greater detail, it isn't as exciting as it appears on the surface. A great example here is foods that claim to be '90% fat free'. Is this a good thing? What's the typical benchmark for these types of products? Of course, 90% fat free may be a good selling point for fried chips, but if it was milk for example, regular full-fat milk only has about 4-5% fat, so '90% fat free' suddenly would sound much less appealing for anyone looking to count calories. Another example: 'up to 50% off". This could mean just 1% off on most items or no discount at all. The lesson here is that yes, large numbers used in headlines can easily grab attention, just don't automatically accept data at face value or let the initial headline stir your emotions; be prepared to interrogate it until you are comfortable with it in the context of your decision-making situation.

Following on from this, don't be afraid to ask questions if you don't understand something. Many different organisations have many different ways of describing things, and much as we would all like to pretend that we know it all (even those of us who have a few years of experience behind us), we don't. So be prepared to put away your ego and ask. Don't be afraid to dig into data or the definitions of terms which are presented to you, so that you can understand what they truly represent. "Do those numbers represent volume sales or value sales?" "By volume sales, do you mean volume of units sold or something else?" Having the humility to admit you would like some help in understanding something can also really open opportunities to you: opportunities to speed up your learning, of course; opportunities to forge working bonds with people you ask for help (it can be flattering to show someone you value their expertise); and frequently others will thank you for helping them understand better by asking the questions they were too timid to ask.

SUMMARY

- Too much choice can increase anxiety over making the perfect choice; yet perfection is impossible.

- Good enough will often set you apart from the procrastinators.

- Consider applying the progressive/legal/moral test to get you moving.

- You have the power to decide; your organisation wants you to use it, your future depends upon you using it.

- Get more comfortable making decisions by being able to justify why you are making them.

- Accept that you will make mistakes; most of them will not end your world, but turn out to be great learning opportunities.

- Simple risk evaluation can help you to see what you could do to reduce the likelihood or impact of failure.

- Ensure you understand the data you have; be objective and beware of bias.

CHAPTER 5

THE ART & SCIENCE OF GETTING THINGS DONE

The previous chapter on making decisions highlighted a key part of our journey on making any progress at all – making choices that would guide us along our journey on whichever project we undertake. But though making decisions gets us going, to actually make anything happen, we must recognise it's only the start of any chain of events. To put it into context, I'd like to start with a little riddle:

Once upon a time there were three frogs, sitting on a log enjoying the pleasant summer sun. The first frog decided she was getting a little too warm and so decided to jump off so she could have a refreshing swim in the cool lily pond.

How many frogs were left sitting on the log?

If you answered 'two', you'd be wrong. How is this? Well, the first frog had only *decided* to jump off… *but she hadn't actually done it yet*. OK, a bad project management joke I know, but one that illustrates very well the difference between planning to do something and actually getting it done – action!

THE IMPORTANCE OF RESULTS

You will find that for all of the wonderful insight, strategising and planning that is carried out at work, one thing is consistently valued above all others: achieving results, getting things done, making things happen – or as we could say, effecting some kind of change. Early on in our careers, we may simply be responsible for getting our own work done (being what's termed 'individual contributors'), while later on we may be responsible for helping groups of other people to reach their goals whether that be from a management or facilitation point of view.

When it comes down to it, planning is a pointless task if there are no subsequent actions that support the plan's goals. While some industries may say they look beyond only the results and focus on the way in which those results are achieved, they still require some level of results in order to have the luxury of being in that position (in much the same way that for us to consider luxuries on a long-term basis, we must at least have our basic survival level needs met). Therefore, the ability to get things done and produce results is an essential foundation of supporting everything else that we may aspire to do. This chapter will give you a solid framework for being able to manage and execute your workload effectively on any given task, as well as making you aware of the beneficial 'side effects' of approaching it in a structured way. Some of the biggest threats to achieving results include the following factors, and we'll look at why they are so critical, plus what you can do to avoid getting trapped by them:

- Not having a reason 'why'.

- Having no objectives (or unclear ones).

- Loss of motivation and momentum.

- Lack of organisation.

ONCE AGAIN, "WHY?"

As we saw when examining change itself, having a 'why' accomplishes several things – giving you a reason to begin, and giving others a reason to support you. When you are working with others, make sure they understand why your project (or the task) is so important – not just to you, but also to them, the wider organisation or the bigger picture. But having a defined 'why' can also help beyond the initial phase. Pausing from time to time to remember and reiterate the 'why' can help reinforce the belief and momentum, reignite the drive and prevent tasks from drifting or becoming forgotten about as their memory is crowded out by the next noisy priority.

CLEAR OBJECTIVES

A lack of clear objectives can also be one of the easily adopted excuses for both ourselves and others to do a half-hearted job and perhaps not follow through to the genuine level of completion required. But even with the best will, if we are not clear about what must be accomplished, then what is created may simply turn out to be unfit for the purpose for which we need it. A new model of car that has been developed with a huge engine and top-end suspension may have faster acceleration and better handling performance at speed over its predecessor model, but if the need was to create a car with an improved safety record then we have wasted our time on the wrong type of improvement effort. It is also very easy for people to get so caught up in the excitement and passion of a new venture that part way through their focus on the detail leads them in directions that do not support the original defined goal.

Making sure that objectives are clear and understood by all tasked with carrying them out is vital, as is the occasional review to check that activity is still focused in directions that will aid realisation of the defined goal. Further, at an individual task level, most of us are so busy that it is all too easy and tempting for people to take the path of least resistance; if you give them the excuse to ignore or overlook (i.e. eliminate) a piece of work from their schedule, most people will take it. Not necessarily because they don't want to help you, but usually because they are managing by inertia; with so many requests and tasks to accomplish, only those that are continually put at the front of the priority queue get done. And without occasional reminders and clarity of what's required, things that could be regarded as 'other people's problems' are easily shuffled down the pecking order. This is also referred to as 'the squeaky wheel gets the oil' syndrome – attention is paid to the things that demand it. For our own objectives our minds will keep required tasks at the front of our minds while those that don't support our personal goals are, without amplification or repetition, moved out of the way, so when involving colleagues in your projects, maintain regular communication with them, and be able to reiterate the objectives concisely and the 'why' behind them every now and then.

Ensuring that you and everyone else know exactly what must be achieved helps to answer a lot of the questions that you will have in figuring out how to carry out the work (so it will enable decision making and reduce the impact of ambiguity as a potential obstacle). Plus, having a clear objective also links the 'why' to reality. It gives a solid definition of what must be delivered in order to fulfil the 'why', and what tasks and activities must happen.

Without clear objectives, there is a tacit suggestion that the project isn't really important, or at least for other people it suggests that "If it's not important enough to you to be thorough in your preparation and enablement of your team, then it's not important to me and I can prioritise other tasks ahead of it." It pays to avoid the tendency to assume that everyone else's priorities are going to be the same as yours. We know they don't perceive the world in the same way you do, so of course they will need some help to see how important your goals really are to the common good of everyone in your organisation!

TO ASSUME MAKES AN ASS OUT OF U AND ME

While we're on the topic of helping to ensure agreed actions get carried out, it would be fair to expand a little more. As you have control over many decisions and actions that can shape your life, so you should use that ability to ensure that things you have agreed with others get done in a timely manner. Merely assuming they will, even if they have said they will, is setting yourself up for failure. Bearing in mind the difficulty we have staying focused on our own goals, we can imagine how easy it is for us to deprioritise the requests of others unless the burning reason why they are important is kept in our minds. I find assumption of task completion is a similar 'crime' to those of omission of important contextual information or lack of follow-up on a communication to make sure it has been received and correctly understood. At best, it suggests that we couldn't be bothered to put in that little extra effort, and as a result our lack of attention can easily trip us up when we come back to it and expect everything to have worked perfectly without any attendance, supervision or care. When no attempts are made to test them or see if there are any more solid foundations on which to base them, assumptions are a lazy way to make decisions as in reality we are making a guess and frequently adding too much of our own baseless stories to justify finishing our own task, when we could have dug a little deeper or confirmed a few things and made sure. As we saw with justification, it's no crime to make decisions based on what scant evidence we do have, even if we cannot get our hands on much; it is a metaphorical crime when we couldn't be bothered to check whether there ever was any evidence available.

MOTIVATION AND MOMENTUM

Finding your 'why' is usually the key to finding that burst of motivation that drives you to begin. But be aware that this initial spark of enthusiasm is a delicate thing that must be nurtured throughout the course of the project until the very end point has been reached, otherwise it will dwindle and dim, and the project risks losing your interest. This is especially true for longer projects, where constant work on the same area may get tedious and at times test your ability to maintain that required level of motivation, allowing new, fresher and more novel thoughts to take precedence in your mind.

If the project was a particularly large one, then you may also have been faced with the spectre of doubt as to whether you could possibly achieve all that. Despite having been able to get started, this fear of 'will I ever finish this?" can easily return when the project faces delays (remember the valley of death?). This can lead to discomfort and as we have seen earlier in the way our minds work, these kinds of situations can quickly turn into a threat. This means we can end up avoiding the uncomfortable issue, often procrastinating or running away from making further decisions or taking further action, leading to delays and possibly abandonment of the project altogether – in effect choosing the freeze or flight options in order to avoid the perceived growing danger.

We can sometimes feel like there is just so much to do that we are too overawed to even begin as we believe we will definitely fail. So we avoid it. And the longer we avoid it, the worse the anxiety gets – both in our heads, and augmented by reality as we see the available time we have to complete it slowly disappear. It's a vicious circle of negativity.

So here's a trick. Break things down. Into. Very. Small. Steps.

Continuous Achievement

Chopping projects up into small, individual task-level items can reduce the chances of many of the above threats from occurring in several ways by setting up a virtuous circle of what I call continuous achievement. There is a similar principle, which has long been a popular and effective approach in quality management, called continuous improvement. Continuous improvement treats the process of improving the quality of any given area of focus as a journey made up of many small steps. This works on the premise that whatever is being examined, further improvements will always be possible, and by finding and applying them, an accumulation of many small improvements adds up over time to a very large net improvement overall.

This approach has been shown to be very effective as it removes much of the awe of continually looking at the one huge objective, placing focus and attention on smaller and more manageable elements of the whole and moving rapidly from one to the next. It is in fact a core principle employed by the all-conquering Team GB Cycling set-up while headed by performance director Dave Brailsford, who focused on achieving many continuous, if marginal gains (often as little as 1%) in many different areas which, when combined, culminated in a haul of seven out of the 10 track gold medals available at each of the Beijing and London Olympics, and producing talent such as Sir Chris Hoy, Victoria Pendleton CBE and Sir

Bradley Wiggins, the first ever British cyclist to win the Tour de France.[22] A similar approach was taken by head coach Clive Woodward in preparing the England team which won the 2003 Rugby World Cup in the home of their arch-rivals Australia.[23] Paying attention to detail, not being overawed by the scale of the overall task, but really breaking it down, focusing on each individual effort and getting it done, then moving on to the next, surreptitiously constructing a monumental accomplishment, tiny piece by tiny piece. It provides a constant rhythm or cadence of success that can be used to spur on the next effort. In the light of these victories, it is clear that the deconstructive approach of continuous achievement can be used to harness significant, consistent progress in order to complete even the most ambitious of projects.

One Bite At A Time, One Foot In Front Of The Other

By chopping any project up into bite-sized pieces, we can begin to realise the following benefits that help our momentum:

- It makes the objective appear that much more achievable.

- Being able to focus on the next small task makes the project a whole lot less scary to begin with.

- It breaks up our mental picture of it as one almighty challenge and gives it back to us in parts that we can feel a lot more confident about being able to complete, lowering our perceived threat alert and the consequential avoidance reactions that often follow.

Some people find that grouping several individual tasks to represent significant stages of progress and celebrating those can have just as beneficial an effect. In project management these are called milestones and can be good points at which to gather teams together for a quick confidence-reinforcing group hi-five. Milestones also work for me, but at a personal level, on a daily basis I have found the individual task-level checklist to be an incredibly effective technique – in the end it's about trying it out and finding what works best for you.

I have used the methodology in all kinds of circumstances, from large commercial projects to accomplishing monthly objectives, to getting myself fit enough to enter (and survive) a three-day adventure race in the space of about three months. This race involved two and a half days of running, mountain biking and, at times, canoeing through mountainous territory against the clock and about 70 other teams. Having been an occasional ball sports enthusiast to that point in my life (so conditioned for short intense bursts of exercise, not distance), and not having done any regular exercise for several years, I found it tough at first, but was able to get to a level quickly where I was enjoying training thanks to the belief that I could always manage one more step. Turning this mantra over and over in my mind with every footfall, I became a bit of a distance zombie, zoned out for most of the run, but the focus allowed me to eliminate many of the feelings of pain and tiredness, plus the fear of whether or not I could complete longer and longer distances. Telling myself that I only had to take the next step each time and knowing that I always could, I was able to immerse myself in a repetitive cycle of continuous achievement: action, recognition, belief, action, recognition, belief. Facing many more experienced and better prepared teams, in our first year in the competition our team completed all of the stages within the allocated time, finished in a respectable halfway position, and more importantly both survived intact and enjoyed the test.

I also came back from the mountains with a renewed sense of self-confidence, and in further reflecting on my training and application efforts realised I was undergoing experiences very similar to a state of mind that Professor Mihaly Csikszentmihalyi has studied for a great number of years, which it is understood can generate feelings of enjoyment, competence and efficacy. In the field of positive psychology it is referred to as 'flow', and is likened to the state which high-performing exponents of their activity get into when they are focusing solely on the task in hand. Assuming the conditions for flow are there – clarity of goals, immediate feedback and good balance between the perceived difficulty of the task and the perceived capability of the person performing it – Csikszentmihalyi has found that it delivers great benefits in terms of improving personal satisfaction drawn from performance of the activity and attainment of even a small degree of progress as a result of the practice.[24]

While psychologists and neuroscientists continue to explore the exact mechanisms of how flow appears to do this, I would suggest that it may be partly due to the feelings of control over our destiny it can engender in us. Whether illusory or not, I believe that making our tasks appear more achievable, then going out and proving it, and at the end recognising our success has a positive effect on our capacity to take on new challenges with a positive outlook. Our anxiety levels have been reduced, as even by a tiny degree the worries of what might possibly happen (and go wrong) with which we fill our knowledge gaps in new projects or experiences are filled in with solid proof, evidence that we are capable of achieving our goals. This is the basis for confidence and being brave enough to take another small step – something which it would be reasonable to believe is within our capabilities.

Breaking a project down also provides us with many more opportunities to celebrate our progress as we go. The importance of this should not be underestimated as logging and recognising these are a great way to reinforce the fact that what you are doing is working and so should be continued! Patting yourself on the back when mini-targets are hit can improve satisfaction in this way, and are also a good time to remind yourself of the reason why you are doing it. So, having more bite-sized chunks gives you valid opportunities to increase the repetition of these morale-boosting moments.

In his book *What's Stopping You?* author Robert Kelsey recommends keeping a daily diary as it provides evidence of your progress that you can look back upon to give you a morale boost in this way.[25] His focus is very much on encouraging people to escape common feelings of inadequacy and failure and reach their goals simply by taking continuous action and recording it. A diary in which every day you list the two or three next tasks on a specific project that you are going to get done today allows you to focus on only your very next, achievable steps, with only an occasional glance at longer term objectives to ensure that those actions are taking you in the right direction. Some people advocate aiming to accomplish five tasks at a time, some say that any more than three is diluting your focus and setting yourself up to finish none of them. Whether you choose one, three or five, and focus on achieving all of them or accepting that you will complete some of them, it's up to you to find out what works for you.

Like the diary, this is essentially what a good project plan can also do – though there is an aspect of recording progress and detail that many project managers who have come fresh from official methodology training courses forget. While being thorough enough is good, it's not essential to ensure that every single element of the theoretical project management system they are following is fully utilised and rigorously examined, detailed and adhered to all the time. The goal itself is not to produce a glorious, highly complex, all-singing, all-dancing Technicolor project plan. It's to achieve the objective of the project. Sometimes that requires a lot of detail, sometimes it doesn't need as much. Trying to log every single element of every project down to the tiniest of minutiae for every project you encounter is itself difficult to manage, and can easily create a sense of failure and demotivation if even the smallest element is not completed or missed. The project plan is simply a tool that can enable us to serve up the next manageable and relevant set of tasks easily (the few next small steps in the right direction), which we feel capable of focusing on and achieving each day.

Nevertheless, once again we can tip our hat to the power of writing things down. It not only makes it easier to organise, focus on and check off small groups of tasks, but thanks to its recorded nature, it also gives us the chance to look back over time and see those accumulated successes made more real. I have noticed this effect not only when managing projects, but also when updating my CV. Taking a little time to log, define and reflect on what I have accomplished over the given period of time reminds me what I am truly capable of and gives me a massive confidence boost and extra drive to keep going. And by increasing repetition of something that is helping us to set and attain our goals, we also lay the foundations for embedding it as a routine part of what we consider our new 'normality' and making it a habit.

Getting Into The Habit

The late Jim Rohn, entrepreneur and motivational speaker on personal development, had these words to offer on the subject:

*"Motivation is what gets you started.
Habit is what keeps you going."* [26]

Given our understanding that frequent application of effort is the key to achieving large goals, it makes sense that being able to embed (i.e. make automatic) our will to apply ourselves to it would help us not to miss out on doing so. Forming a habit means that we have been able to programme our minds to stop pausing to analyse and evaluate whether or not we should do something, and automatically accept that we should. This of course can be a problem if the habit relates to activities which could be hazardous to our health, such as drugs or other detrimental addictions. But understood, it can also be used to help us. The power of habit is incredibly strong. My parents once commented on actually being pleased to be woken up as I returned from a night out at 3 o'clock in the morning, as they could hear me brushing my teeth, a healthy habit to get into and one which most of us can automatically repeat daily without fail, despite even the willpower-sapping effects of alcohol, exhaustion and sleep deprivation.

Over the last few years I have even managed to incorporate a few minutes of freezing cold shower as a daily habit after reading that it would help my muscles recover from exercise more quickly (I spent a few years adventure racing). I had a good reason to try it out (a strong 'why') reinforced by both research and word of mouth from some of my more experienced peers (so fairly well justified), had the opportunity to do it at least once a day, and whether the placebo effect or otherwise, was willing to embrace the belief that it was having a beneficial effect on my muscles as well as several other physiological and mental side benefits. So in being able to see regular results, I was continually able to reinforce my belief and reason to keep doing it, maintaining my momentum until it became a habit. I don't run any more, but still do it every day.

DIZZY WITH DISORGANISATION

By creating several smaller, more achievable pieces of work you have already begun to organise things in some way, giving them a structure that allows you to use them to a better degree. But in creating many smaller tasks, you have seemingly increased the number of plates that you need to keep spinning. Surely this isn't helping us to manage our work as much as we thought? The benefits of breaking things down far outweigh the negatives, all we need to do is ensure we have an effective way of structuring and organising these many smaller tasks, and this is where a few simple project management methods come in really handy. So here we go with a simple project management checklist – stages you should consider, and aspects of those stages that it is at least good to be aware of:

- Objectives
- Work Breakdown Structure
- Schedule

If you did nothing more than define each of these before you began taking action, you would have made your life much easier already. Here's the low-down on each stage, what you need to know to be able to use it and how it helps you to organise your project.

Objectives

Lay out your objectives. Define exactly what it is that you are trying to achieve. People often use the acronym SMART for their objectives to try and make them more achievable.

SMART stands for:

- *Specific* – what exactly are you trying to do? The more general you make your objective, the more difficulty you will have in knowing if you have really reached your goal. Vagueness doesn't just make it difficult to confirm what it was that you were trying to do, it opens the door for you or others to cheat in claiming that it could be interpreted as having been completed… 'from a certain point of view'. When you get into this habit, your focus is moved away from achieving something that benefits the organisation to a focus on simply being able to demonstrate that you did… something – ticking a box for its own sake. Savvy managers will see through this and challenge you on it, you will end up with egg on your face as you try to justify something which didn't really add much value, and it doesn't end up helping anyone. So get specific – make sure you know what you want to achieve and why that is going to be of benefit.

- *Measurable* – if it can't be measured, it can't be managed – just make sure that you are measuring the right things. By measuring, you can tell when you have got to where you were aiming for. This can be in terms of direct quantities ('our target is one million unit sales in South Africa') or even time ('make sure that the business is still operating in the education market by the end of 2015'). Then there is measurement of quality. Quality can be harder to measure, but you should seek to try as best you can. How do you measure customer satisfaction for instance? Well, in the absence of hard direct data, you can apply a representative measure. So, number of customer complaints received per week could be a measure of this. Or number of incorrect deliveries reported. Or you could base your measurements upon surveys and polls of your customers themselves. Asking them a number of relevant questions about their experience as a customer and analysing the results can give both overall scores to measure and grade against (a Customer Satisfaction Index, if you will) but it can also provide a deep enough level of detail to allow you to see the performance of specific aspects of customer service activity.

- *Achievable* – try to ensure that the size of objective you set yourself is realistic. It does no one any good to set yourself up to fail from the start by taking on something that is obviously unachievable. Resource is often wasted pursuing the impossible dream, and you will feel pretty bad when the time to review progress or final result comes around.

- *Relevant* – ensure that the objectives of your project are going to contribute towards improving your situation. Even if part of the strategy requires some areas to get worse in order that others can get better, to the outsider it may seem like a backwards step, but if you are able to demonstrate how it is necessary for achievement of the overall project goal, then it could be worth setting as an objective.

- *Time-bound* – along with measuring the result, measure the time it takes or should take to complete the project. Do this in two ways: your original estimate (called a baseline), and the actual reality as you move through the project work.

Be prepared for the fact that your initial thoughts re: expected outcomes (both in terms of direct measurable result, and the time and resource you think it should have taken to complete them) may be wrong to some degree. As we have seen previously, this is a natural part of trying to predict the future, or as it is often called, forecasting. What we do is put down what seems reasonable at first and adjust as we understand more. Get good first and improve later.

Work Breakdown Structure

After establishing our objectives, we can build a Work Breakdown Structure (WBS). This is exactly what it sounds like: a list of individual tasks that need to be carried out to fulfil the overall objective. When building a Work Breakdown Structure, you may wish to include every task level activity required. You can consolidate several tasks into similar groups later (milestones) in order to review the entire project in fewer, larger chunks, but for detailed tracking purposes you may wish to write down all tasks which will require a specific person to carry out a specific activity.

To make sure you list all of the tasks and don't miss any out by accident, it may be wise to describe the project process step by step, and for each step write down the action that must be taken, whether a physical action, or making a decision. This is called process mapping, and can help you to organise the tasks in the correct order. Many organisations have developed processes once upon a time to meet specific requirements, but never formally documented the process or any changes to it that may have occurred over time, so it can be a real eye-opener to see what actually happens now and not simply what everyone thinks is supposed to happen. Having the process visually portrayed makes it both easier to understand how the process works and easier to spot opportunities to improve the process, such as removing parts of it that don't make sense or may no longer be required. Having redundant process elements is not uncommon, and clues that they may be present include people responding to questions about why the process exists with answers like, "Because that's the way we've always done it." Whenever you hear this, be sure to challenge it by asking questions to understand why it was originally put in place, and whether or not there is still a valid reason for having it in the process.

Sometimes, if planning a process that doesn't yet exist (common in projects attempting something new for the organisation), then asking others for their input on what might constitute a good, comprehensive task list can come in useful. Utilising colleagues' mental effort to help in this way is very similar to brainstorming in that it allows several different points of view to be focused on the challenge, increasing the chances that a comprehensive list is generated and fewer important elements missed. Involving colleagues who execute the process (and so can be considered subject matter experts on it) also brings to the table highly relevant understanding of issues whose consideration may be essential to the project's success. I elaborate on how to brainstorm effectively in the chapter on imagination, but suffice to say utilising this technique can often capture many more elements of which tasks might need to be completed that a single individual hadn't considered on their own. So, let's use an example to put the elements of building a WBS into practice. If we were planning to bake a cake, the task list we generated might look something like this (in no particular order):

- Mix ingredients of cake batter.

- Get a recipe book.

- Get required materials ready.

- Read recipe book (to understand all of the processes and materials that will be required, including amount of time needed).

- Leave cake to cool.

- Once the oven is warm enough, cook cake for 40 minutes.

- Put the cake mixture into a cake tin.

- Put the cake tin in the oven.

- Eat the cake.

- Take cake out of the oven.

- Decorate the cake.

- Turn the oven on and leave to warm up for 15 minutes.

- Serve the cake.

Of course this is currently just a pile of the tasks listed in an order that makes no sense, so the next step is to schedule them into the correct order, giving us a logical Work Breakdown Structure as follows. I find that writing each step down on a separate post-it note and rearranging on a wall, desktop or board makes this part of the planning process both easier and more fun.

Scheduling The Work Breakdown Structure: Baking A Cake

1. Get a recipe book.

2. Read recipe book (to understand all of the processes and materials that will be required, including amount of time needed).

3. Get required materials ready.

4. Mix ingredients of cake batter.

5. Put the cake batter into a cake tin.

6. Turn the oven on and leave to warm up for 15 minutes.

7. Put the cake tin in the oven.

8. Leave to bake for 40 minutes.

9. Take cake out of the oven.

10. Leave cake to cool.

11. Decorate the cake.

12. Serve the cake.

13. Eat the cake.

If we estimate how long each task will take, then viewed in a linear fashion, where each task is accomplished in sequence, we can get an idea of how long baking a cake might take from start to finish. As already alluded to, seeing a process map can offer insights as to how it can be improved. Some of these tasks may require their predecessors to finish before the next step can commence, but not all of them. If it takes 15 minutes to mix the ingredients and put the mixture into a tin, then we could move step 7 (Turn the oven on) to earlier in the list – making it the new step 4. By doing so, we can initiate the warming up sub-process which takes 15 minutes so that it runs in parallel with the 15 minutes required to mix and put it into a tin. By the time we have completed these steps, the oven will be warm enough to put the cake straight in and begin step 8 – cooking. We have just saved ourselves 15 minutes.

Deciding and scheduling tasks which could run parallel with one another is called setting dependencies. Turning the oven on doesn't require that any of the previous steps be completed before we do it; we would of course be wasting more power than we needed to by turning it on at the very start, but just seeing the order of things makes it a lot easier for us to judge where we could optimise our project process and how. Having your Work Breakdown Structure laid out in process map fashion frees up your mind from having to juggle the entire concept, all of its elements and dynamics, so that you can concentrate on optimising the sequence – yet more evidence of the power of writing things down.

Once we have our schedule, we'll need to identify what resources might be required, both from a cash and materials point of view, and also from a skills or abilities point of view; can we manage to accomplish all of this ourselves, or will other people and or skills be required?

Working through the project in this manner, we will quickly find that we now have a list of tasks that need to be accomplished, we have a good idea of how long the entire project is likely to take, and we can begin to work on the tasks or assign them to others if required.

Let Them See It Coming

If other people's input and effort is necessary, or the project is likely to affect them in some way, then as expressed in the chapter on change, making people aware of things in advance is usually a much more effective method than springing a surprise on them. Unexpected workload requests are often met (at least initially) with rejection as they are in effect changes to the requestee's planned schedule and thus will cause discomfort that the requestee will try to resist (fight) or avoid (flight) or worse, accept but not act upon (freeze), making you think everything is going fine when in reality it is not. Involving those people in the initial project planning can be a good way of reducing the resistance to sudden change, and involving them in the brainstorming session for your WBS can also reduce resistance further as when assignment occurs, it will be even more familiar to them if they have had a hand in creating it, and you will have more time to identify and manage any issues that do arise early in the planning process.

Tracking Progress & Accountability

When working with groups, detailed assignment logging is vital, as without it, tasks will sit on the list of things to do, but never get done by anyone. Here's a short story about four people named Everybody, Somebody, Anybody and Nobody that illustrates the point nicely:

There was an important job to be done and Everybody was sure that Somebody would do it. Anybody could have done it, but Nobody did it. Somebody got angry about that because it was Everybody's job. Everybody thought that Anybody could do it, but Nobody realised that Everybody wouldn't do it. It ended up that Everybody blamed Somebody when Nobody did what Anybody could have done.

Not taking the time to assign tasks and actions sadly leads to this state of affairs all too easily. You will no doubt encounter this in many meetings throughout your career (I know I have), but knowing this, you now have the chance to shine as somebody who can organise and help such groups to get results.

Whether you are assigning tasks from your Work Breakdown Structure or simply recapping on actions agreed in a meeting, here is a framework that you can use to clarify what is required, and by whom it will be done. Ensure it is clear what the expected deliverable is in each task in order for it to be completed, by when this has to be completed, and then detail for each one the following roles, collectively known as the RACI model:

- Responsible – this is the person who should be doing the work required on the task. It is their responsibility to complete that task.

- Accountable – this is the person who takes ownership for the ultimate achievement of the task. They may not be doing the work themselves but do have responsibility for ensuring that the person responsible for a specific task is able to carry it out and does so. Often the Accountable person can be a manager and may be accountable for ensuring completion of a specific group of tasks within the same project (though on smaller projects the Responsible and Accountable roles might be assigned to the same person). Even though they may not report to the project manager and may even be technically higher in the organisation's reporting hierarchy, you could regard them almost as a sub-project manager accountable for ensuring completion of a specific chunk of the project.

- Consulted – who should be consulted during the task? Typically, this might be a subject matter expert who can deliver advice and insights that the people planning and carrying out the project work should be aware of. The term subject matter expert could also include stakeholders and not just experts of a particular topic – people who will be affected by the project, as their area of expertise could be the dynamics of their working environment, both currently and in a future state if and when the project is completed.

- Informed – usually these are simply the stakeholders – people who may be impacted by the result of the project or task, or even by the work that is being carried out, and who should be informed of any progress or changes.

RACI models are useful as they keep it simple. This version maps the RACI functions required for each task to specific people. Several functions could be assigned to the same person, or the same function such as C or I could be assigned to several people; try not to assign the R or A function to multiple people or they may each expect the other person to shoulder the load. The goal is to ensure whoever reads it can get a quick and clear understanding of exactly what must be done and who must do it or be included in the task.

Role-based RACI matrix example

Task	Responsible	Accountable	Consulted	Informed
Research Technology	IT Specialist	IT Manager	Process Owner	Project Manager
Build Plan	Project Manager	IT Director	IT Specialist	Project Team
Approve Plan	IT Director	IT Director	Project Manager	Project Team
Communicate Plan	Project Manager	IT Director	IT Director	Project Team

This matrix improves team productivity by clarifying and reducing possible confusion. It also makes it easier for whoever is managing the project to quickly know with whom they need to follow up in order to track progress, address potential problems and achieve the goal in good time. When shared with project teams and stakeholders, it also keeps that cadence of continuous achievement visible to everyone involved so that successes can be celebrated and momentum can be maintained. As always, when following up with other people who may not have performed as expected, remember that they are human and subject to a myriad of unexpected influences, so be open to understanding their situations instead of just jumping down their throats. Try to identify and understand what factors may have prevented them from accomplishing the tasks on time, and be objective in efforts to figure out how to overcome them.

Effective Meeting Management

To round off this chapter, I will stay in the realm of meetings as these are probably one of the most common ways in which companies expend effort without achieving results.

With the RACI model, you are now armed with a simple matrix to help ensure any actions agreed or even just discussed as a good idea within a meeting get defined, delegated and accomplished. This alone is likely to mark you out in many organisations as a highly competent employee who gets results, but in terms of general meeting etiquette and dynamics, there are a number of ways in which you can also stand out as someone who helps to make effective use of the time of anyone else who is present in your meetings. With experience, some people and working groups become adept at assuming these roles without a formal declaration to the attendees, but for the most part, it is both effective and necessary to assign these roles at the start of each one. I have lost count of the number of meetings I have attended which could have benefited from some kind of role assignment at the outset or before they convened.

Here's another tip: before calling a meeting, ensure that you and everyone else knows why you are having it. What is the meeting objective? It may be to make a final decision on a big project, or it may simply be to introduce and explore the initial concept of something you are thinking about doing. Will you exchange feedback or even extra ideas from a quick brainstorm before expending further effort, or do you expect the decision to be confirmed or finalised during the meeting? You may need people to prepare or think about certain issues in advance, or you may intend that most of the thinking work is done in the meeting itself – more of a workshop.

remember that they are human and subject to a myriad of unexpected influences, so be open to understanding their situations instead of just jumping down their throats. Try to identify and understand what factors may have prevented them from accomplishing the tasks on time, and be objective in efforts to figure out how to overcome them.

Effective Meeting Management

To round off this chapter, I will stay in the realm of meetings as these are probably one of the most common ways in which companies expend effort without achieving results.

With the RACI model, you are now armed with a simple matrix to help ensure any actions agreed or even just discussed as a good idea within a meeting get defined, delegated and accomplished. This alone is likely to mark you out in many organisations as a highly competent employee who gets results, but in terms of general meeting etiquette and dynamics, there are a number of ways in which you can also stand out as someone who helps to make effective use of the time of anyone else who is present in your meetings. With experience, some people and working groups become adept at assuming these roles without a formal declaration to the attendees, but for the most part, it is both effective and necessary to assign these roles at the start of each one. I have lost count of the number of meetings I have attended which could have benefited from some kind of role assignment at the outset or before they convened.

Here's another tip: before calling a meeting, ensure that you and everyone else knows why you are having it. What is the meeting objective? It may be to make a final decision on a big project, or it may simply be to introduce and explore the initial concept of something you are thinking about doing. Will you exchange feedback or even extra ideas from a quick brainstorm before expending further effort, or do you expect the decision to be confirmed or finalised during the meeting? You may need people to prepare or think about certain issues in advance, or you may intend that most of the thinking work is done in the meeting itself – more of a workshop.

Either way, there are no cast iron rules on what you can and can't call a meeting for, just be sure to let everyone you invite know what you are trying to achieve beforehand so that they can get their brains in the right gear in advance. This will help to make the meeting more productive from the start and avoid what everyone thought was a short meeting suddenly spilling into a sudden emergency workshop effort. The core roles that you may wish to assign are:

- *Chairperson* – this person is responsible for keeping the content of the meeting relevant to the original topic of the meeting. If people begin to discuss a matter that is too far away from the meeting objective, then the chairperson has the right to let everyone know that this matter should be logged for later discussion so that the immediate discussion can return to making progress on the pre-agreed meeting objective.

- *Scribe* – a note taker; different meetings may require different levels of note taking. I have learnt that due to the human mind's capacity to make sense of words which lack many letters, simply due to their context I can speed type, and even though the initial transcript looks appallingly poor in terms of spelling, I can practically capture word for word everything that was said, and easily and quickly correct it after the meeting has ended. This method does have the tendency to focus the scribe's attention on getting the words down, reducing their ability to participate fully in the meeting from a subject evaluation point of view, so be aware of this. For most meetings though, simply capturing summary minutes in bullet format should suffice, these include:

    ◊ Who attended the meeting.

    ◊ When it was held.

    ◊ What the topic of discussion/meeting objective was.

    ◊ Bullet points of salient topics or points made, and any actions that have been agreed (with RACI details and agreed completion dates). All actions as per our project Work

Breakdown Structure should include an exact description of what is to be done, by when, and by whom.

The role of scribe often feels like an imposition – the job that no one in the meeting really wants as it requires them to write things down and actually do some work when everyone else may be coasting (or hiding). But in reality, it's one of the most important roles in terms of ensuring that each meeting has a progressive effect on the project in question. By making use of the power of writing things down, it removes ambiguity, provides a captured reference for future work, and avoids having to have repeated meetings in the future about the same issues which get discussed and discussed but for some reason that no one can quite put their finger on, are never acted upon.

- *Timekeeper* – just having someone call out to all present key time milestones can really help the chairperson to bring the meeting back on track before too much irrelevant discussion takes place and make the most of the time the group has together. At one company, because so many speakers in our annual internal review meetings consistently overstepped their allocated time slot, one year we set up a system of traffic lights manned by the finance director (to lend them more authority). He would turn the lights to amber with five minutes to go, encouraging the speaker to wrap up their topic. Once they reached red he would also sound a buzzer and the speaker had to stop there and then, parking any other areas they hadn't covered for later discussion. It sounds a bit draconian, but after the first couple of speakers had received this treatment it focused the minds of the remaining presenters quite well, sessions began to adhere to the planned schedule a lot more than in the past and became a lot more concise (meaning more people stayed awake and were able to actually listen to what was said).

SUMMARY

- Planning is of little value without action.

- Be clear and concise with requests to others.

- Be ready to follow up on progress of agreed actions – don't blindly assume everything will be complete at the deadline.

- Apply a continuous achievement approach to make larger, more complex projects seem easier.

- Taking action is one of the best ways of making you feel better about your goals and maintaining momentum.

- Don't overlook the power of writing things down – use Work Breakdown Structures to help you organise and manage tasks.

- Use RACI model to help track and ensure completion of tasks.

- Don't be afraid to manage your meetings – it will save everyone a lot of time.

CHAPTER 6
IMAGINATION

I have always found that if unsure of the way ahead, an imaginative person can always come up with some options or possibilities of what could be done. In his book *A Whole New Mind* author Dan Pink suggests we are entering a new age of work, characterised by increased value being placed on "high concept" aptitudes such as the ability to detect patterns and opportunities and gain new insights by "combining seemingly unrelated ideas into something new."[27]

THE 'GOD' ELEMENT?

Imagination it would seem, one of the most powerful and innate skills we are blessed with, can help us develop these aptitudes to find new, innovative ways of doing things and help us to figure things out by looking at them from new perspectives. In essence, because of its seeming lack of limitations and almost infinite capacity for creativity it could be termed the 'God Element' of our thinking.

And so, I see imagination as being vital to your work life, a major part of which will centre around figuring things out, often in new situations. This will be even more pronounced if you make constant progress in your career – simply as a result of the learning curve involved in taking a new position, you will be continuously encountering new situations and scenarios which will require decisions and action to resolve.

MENTAL MAPS & CONCEPTUAL CONNECTIONS

Our experiences help shape our perception of the world and build our metaphorical 'mental maps' – the frameworks on which we base our understandings, belief systems and decisions. In his Stanford Presidential Lecture on Analogy as the Core of Cognition, Professor of Cognitive Science Douglas Hofstadter muses on this subject, suggesting that our maps may simply be bundles of individual analogies that we have acquired and assimilated into whatever existing analogies or bundles we already possess.[28] As we grow, we develop new, larger bundle structures into which we assign pieces of information which share certain common aspects that we feel can be classified as being alike. For me, this is simply chunking up – the creation of larger, simpler blocks of information that make it easier for us to move from one concept to another by focusing on their similarities at the expense of ignoring those elements that are not alike.

The critical element here in enabling this continual metamorphosis of growth, perspective and understanding is how we are able to recognise similarities and make these kinds of connections. To do that we have to at least be able to label or define individual units of meaning that pertain to any given thing, be it physical or conceptual. I like to call these units 'mental hooks'. And by increasing the number of hooks we associate with any given piece of information, we increase the number of opportunities to make new connections with other pieces of information so that we may develop more effective understandings and see new patterns thanks to our more sophisticated maps.

Of course, I must add that more sophisticated maps means ones that allow for simpler understanding and effective use of information they contain. Complexity on its own adds no value (we can make anything more complex simply by adding many more variables whether they be highly relevant or not), but by being more effective at mentally accessing (noticing

- What size is it?

- What is its orientation?

- How does it stand/how is it balanced?

- How does it feel? Consistently the same all over?

- How does it sound? Does it make any noise? How frequently does this happen? Does it make a noise when you get closer? What changes about it? What changes about it if certain other things happen?

You can begin to move on to asking more abstract questions, such as:

- What is it not? (OK, you may need to place a limit on your responses to this one, as you could be here forever, but it's worth trying out the question every now and again to see what answers you get.)

- What is it like? In what way? What else is it like?

- What does it have in common with other things?

- What is its purpose? (In what context? In the context of this exercise? Or the general context of being a candle? What do candles do? Can you think of any other contexts that might apply?)

Now that you've begun to explore its properties from a host of different perspectives, keep going. Try posing new types of questions that allow you to interrogate the properties of the candle in new ways, for example:

- What groups of things might it be described as belonging to/sharing some of the same characteristics as?

- Does it change? How, and over what period of time?

- What about its stability?

- What is likely to happen if something else happens to it or around it?

- For how long would you expect it to exist if nothing new happens?

- What effect does the candle have on its surroundings?

- In how many ways could you describe each of these observations?

    ◊ e.g. It feels firm. It also feels somewhat dry, though not like chalk. Somewhere in between dry and wet (a good term might be 'waxy', of course).

You could take any point you make or any of the objects, concepts or phrases noted in your observations and begin to interrogate them, taking you to new, unexplored areas of thought. If you have been able to try this out and really get into it, you have at some point probably experienced the feeling of your mind racing faster than you can write. That's OK here, it means you are making new connections and exercising your grey matter. The more observations you write down, the more you will see just how rich a world we live in, and the easier it will become to apply those same interrogations to anything else you encounter. Doing so will give you lots of small insights into their properties, and create lots of new mental 'hooks' for you to enrich your map of the universe, and how things fit together. When you encounter them again, they will not seem so alien or strange, and you will have developed some idea of the dynamics of the item or situation. In addition, you are more likely to have the presence of mind to be able to deal with the situation in a logical and objective way; as you are more likely to recognise what's going on, your mind is less likely to default to its 'this is different, so by default it's a threat' defensive panic mode where objectivity, logic and insight shut down and mental and physical resource is diverted to your fight, flight or freeze response in an attempt to keep you safe.

When applying your observational abilities on a practical basis, you may not have too much time to explore the full gamut of an object or situation's dynamics each time, so here is a short group of highly useful questions that can help give you a fast yet wider understanding of whatever you apply them to. Consider the following '7 Ws' of anything you want to investigate:

- Why?

- What?

- Where?

- When?

- Who?

- hoW? (OK, I cheated a bit on this one just to help the concept fit – call it poetic licence.)

- What if…?

If you practise both of these observational techniques regularly, you will soon see how easy it is to generate mental hooks about anything you observe, massively opening up your scope for linking concepts together and finding innovative ways to solve the challenges you encounter.

As a last note here, once you get into this possibilities mindset, you may find yourself coming up with some useful insights at the most inopportune of moments. If you don't capture those thoughts immediately, they will be forgotten about, so I would recommend keeping either a pen and paper or a mobile device handy in your car and by your bed so that you can write down or type your thoughts for later reference wherever you are, whenever it happens, even if that happens to be the middle of the night. You could even simply send yourself an email when inspiration strikes, just so long as you don't lose that potential moment of quality that your mind has just generated.

Brainstorming – Group Hook Generation At Work

At work, it's not uncommon to see groups of people generating lots of mental hooks in this manner with the intention of finding among them a solution to a specific objective that has been set. This process of generating and collecting multiple ideas to solve a specific challenge is called brainstorming, and while it is possible to do so on your own, it can add a new dimension to include other people in your brainstorm. For one, having a variety of different perspectives and experiences can often increase the chance that you will not miss things due to only applying one way of thinking about any given topic. Secondly, if you are going to be working with others on a project, it can be a good, fun way to involve them early in its initial conception, making the project more familiar to them, and increasing the chances that they will want to give their time and effort to support it during the execution stages.

Brainstorming is an incredibly useful technique for a variety of situations. It is especially effective generating ideas or lists of things. In this case, we are looking to generate a comprehensive list of activities that will allow us to reach a defined goal once they are all completed. It would be amiss of me to talk about such a useful technique without giving you some idea of how to apply it, so here is the basic guide to group brainstorming (because of the group dynamic, there are some slightly different rules to the candle exercise that you might typically conduct on your own). What you'll need:

- Something to log your ideas with (time to utilise the power of writing things down again!). A computer, tablet or mobile device is fine, and will save some paper. Personally, I prefer to use post-it notes, as they make it a little more real, a little more fun and allow you to play with the way you classify the ideas you generate.

- Your brains.

- Some time and a location where preferably you will not be interrupted.

First of all, state what type of list you are trying to compile, what's the goal? (e.g. We are going to build a list of possible names for our new product, or we are going to generate a list of possible taglines for our new advertisement.) For the purposes of our example we are going to build a list of all tasks that we think might be required to bake a cake.

Proceed to write down/type/log each and every idea that springs to mind. Use some of the above questions to stimulate your thinking and help generate new ideas. Now, here's a very important bit: effective brainstorming works best when certain rules are applied. These rules should be stated at the start of every brainstorm session to ensure that all involved recognise and understand them, and even if they have heard or seen them before, it's always handy to remind everyone of them before you begin:

- In a brainstorm session, quantity of ideas is what we are aiming for, not quality. We can sort, evaluate and classify them later on, but now, the sheer volume of ideas logged increases the chances that some of them are likely to be a good fit. Thus, to encourage people to give us plenty of them, we also apply rule number 2:

- All ideas are valid and welcome. No ideas should be judged in any way. Try even to avoid saying "that's a really good idea" as it can colour the way people perceive the other ideas that are being generated. Now is not the time for judgment of any kind except encouragement of generation of more ideas. Any idea generated should be met with "good" or "great" – encouragement not based on anyone's opinion of the idea, but simply on the basis that it is another idea to add to the list. Having some fun and being comfortable laughing at some of the more outlandish ideas can help our brains get into the right kind of relaxed thinking mood to extend them or generate new connections. It is difficult to avoid making judgments of any kind, so it's good to have a nominated chairperson ensure that it doesn't happen, or that any opinions that are made are met with the statement, "That doesn't matter, it's been said so it goes on the board." This rule is most effective when new or creative concepts are being discussed. No matter how outlandish or ridiculous, one spark of any idea could trigger someone to think of another.

- Feel free to build on or amend existing ideas – don't feel like you are copying or ripping off someone else's idea; if you can take it a step further (or even backwards, up, down, or to either side) then that's perfectly OK.

Prepare To Play

So, we've found a way of increasing the number of hooks we have to play with by learning to observe things from different perspectives. But we should also look to improve the ways in which we can utilise and manipulate those hooks to work for us in generating new ideas. On any given subject, if insight is required, I would advocate being prepared to mess around a little, explore and push the limits by asking questions like "What if?" and "Wouldn't it be great if…?"

It's one of the ways in which children learn so much, so quickly – exploration through imaginative play. You can do it on your own, or better still, fertilise your imagination by playing with friends or colleagues if they are comfortable doing so.

I find good 'what if' exercises that help us stretch our understanding of how we define the world include word-play games. One such could be taking some existing concepts such as film names and repurposing them by changing some of the words so that you create a similar sounding (made-up) film name which encapsulates the name of a foodstuff. So for instance, *Jurassic Park* might become Jurassic Tart due to the similarity in sound and syllables. *Slumdog Millionaire* might become Slumhotdog Millionaire, and *Rocky* could become Choccy. As for *Cloudy With A Chance of Meatballs*, well, that one is already there.

These kinds of games and variations on them can get you into the 'possibilities' mindset that is so good for innovative thinking. Lunch breaks are a good time to do this as it's 'your time' and so there is no pressure to look like you are doing 'proper' work. In fact, you *are* doing proper work – by exploring in this way, you are in fact advancing your understanding and encouraging innovation. But by trying them out in a non-pressured period (i.e. where you are not expected to be delivering any results or specific output) you will find yourself truly playing at them, getting into a mindset more conducive to creativity and less likely to succumb to the Sawyer Effect – a phenomenon where creative output productivity slumps once an activity is viewed as an obligation ('work') rather than an intrinsically rewarding pastime in itself. Even if you're just messing around with non-work-related ideas, you are in effect practising and expanding on your grasp of connections and relativity, and through developing your work skills in any relevant way you are doing what Stephen R. Covey refers to as 'sharpening the saw' – developing your own capabilities, one of his 7 Habits Of Highly Effective People.[29]

CHAPTER 6: IMAGINATION

AROUND THE ROADBLOCKS

Playing has an interesting effect on our minds. It reduces anxiety and helps to free us from the blinkered bonds of purely logical thought. When trying to figure out the solution to a particularly tricky problem, such as one that requires some abstract or 'out of the box' thinking, being able to loosen up mentally can help us make connections between distantly related concepts. It allows us to take the necessary backwards steps in our train of thought to see alternative ways around particularly taxing puzzles, the confined dead-end wall which our tunnel-visioned logical thought process may continue to beat our head against, no matter how hard we think. Companies such as Google deliberately make their workplaces fun for this reason as they depend on the generation of new, innovative ideas to keep ahead of the competition – and the technology sector at large is no slouch at this. So, getting into a playful, less serious mindset can help you to relax and more easily access those mental hooks which may seem at first to have only tenuous, yet later on, vital significance to your problem. Oh, and the other great thing about playing – it's great fun!

I have found that among the work environments which I have experienced and observed, the best progress has been made in those in which staff have been encouraged to have some fun in their work. It can put you and your colleagues at ease and into a creative and innovative state of mind, though neuroscientist David Rock suggests another way to access this useful mode of thought, especially useful if you are trying to figure out a particularly challenging problem on your own.[30]

Instead of focusing harder on it (trying to beat it with more logic), by thinking about your thinking processes themselves (i.e. what you are thinking and how you are thinking), you allow your mind to take a step back from the immediate problem that is right in front of you, and increase the chances of being able to see a way around it. Remember chunking up? Thinking at a highly conceptual and low level of detail helps your mind to simplify matters and from there it is more likely that you will be able to find similarities with a larger and more varied range of concepts perhaps generating more options, some of whose hooks loosely match up. It's like mentally stepping back in order to see the bigger picture, a wider set of contextual information.

Direct And Narrative Thought

For some pointers on how to practise accessing this relaxed mental state, in *Your Brain At Work* Rock tells us that most of our normal waking lives are spent in a 'narrative' state of mind, where our minds are occupied by the constant noise of our own thoughts processing incoming information, fitting it into our mental maps of the world, trying to make meaning out of it and utilising it to think about what is going to happen in the future. This is the state where logic rules and it can be difficult to make those loose, abstract connections when also trying to deal with the noise of all the information inputs we are receiving and producing.

He suggests that to quieten the mind, try focusing for 10 seconds on direct sensual stimuli such as the feeling of the seat you are sitting on, the feeling of your own breathing, or the taste of something you have in your mouth. This deactivates the noisy narrative state and activates what he calls the direct experience state which frees up brain effort to mentally manipulate the focus of your attention in more sophisticated ways, thereby giving you more chance of figuring out how to find a solution to your issue. In essence, by being able to quiet and focus the mind we are achieving a state of mindfulness. This highly reflective state is typically present in our early morning waking moments after a good night's sleep and as per Rock's findings, can be activated by stimulation of our senses. This combination may be why I personally find an early morning shower one of the most fruitful times of day for gaining insights and solutions to any particular challenges I currently have.

Mindfulness has been described by many scientists, philosophers and thinkers for thousands of years as the path to being able to focus your attention intently on something, and is frequently used to help you know yourself better. As we see with any opportunity for progress or learning, one of the first steps required for change to happen is awareness of the need for change; having a reason why; simply starting by recognising that there is a problem or opportunity that requires some kind of change. If we can use mindfulness to become more self-aware, then we may be better able to recognise the real problems that confound us or present themselves to us, giving us a much better chance of knowing where to focus our efforts on making progress.

Meditation has been shown to improve a person's ability to be mindful and choose where they focus their attention – whether it be in the narrative world or that of direct experience, depending on which is more suitable at the time. Mindfulness and meditation have also been shown in scientific tests to confer various health benefits associated with reducing anxiety and stress levels. Rock recommends regular (daily) practice to improve your cognitive ability to switch between the narrative and more insightful direct experience modes of thought. Retired mindfulness researcher John Teasdale described mindfulness as a learnable skill, a habit which the more it is practised becomes easier to perform, going as far as suggesting that being mindful is simply "Accessing something we already have. Mindfulness isn't difficult. What's difficult is to remember to be mindful." [31]

IMAGINATION – THE FIFTH UTILITY

I place so much value on how important our imagination is to progress that in addition to describing it as the God Element, I'm also christening it the Fifth Utility (after the first four: water, gas, electricity and more recently IP – internet protocol), as I believe that like the others, it is a ubiquitous yet essential resource for our progress as a species, indeed to our very survival, due to its capacity to shape the world in which we live in any particular way we choose. The exciting thing about imagination is that it is free, abundant and accessible to almost everyone. So it is with this in mind that I would like to explore the concept of utilisation – applying your observations and imagination to practical situations, concepts or objects and their potential uses, enabling you to figure out new possibilities to solve the challenges in front of you.

At a simple level, we could take a simple ruler, of the type that children use at school, and ask the question: What is it used for? Even if we have not been practising collecting generating hooks and conceptual potential, then we can instantly come up with a few obvious answers for its typical uses, such as drawing a straight line, or measuring things using the calibrated scales that most rulers possess. But if we kick our mental hook machines into gear, we can rapidly increase its potential practical uses by asking the question: What *could* it be used for?

A bit like the candle activity, to exercise your utilisation radar you may want to do this once in a while with any random object, concept or thought that takes your fancy.

So, how many possible uses might there be for a common ruler? Well, we can see that it is good for measuring – so it could be used for measuring all sorts of other things. Measuring distances between places might appear a bit impractical, but it could be applied to a map to give us some data to calculate with the map's scale. It has a straight edge, so that could be useful in any number of given situations – still drawing, but lining up blocks, or bricks. It is made of plastic and fairly hard, yet somewhat flexible, so it might be useful in a situation where slapping something could be seen as beneficial – fly swatting for instance (though I am not condoning the mistreatment of living beings in any way). Notice that we are not restricting ourselves by searching for its best role or optimum usage situation, nor judging whether it would be the absolute best tool for the job. But in employing the principle of 'good enough', we are recognising whether it could be relatively effective, especially if there were no alternatives.

What we're doing is seeing beyond the uses that we have been conditioned to look out for, and by observing the ruler's properties at a purely utilitarian level, we are making it easier for ourselves to recognise other applications in which those properties might be useful. We are creating and matching mental hooks. If we get a little more imaginative, we could really begin to let loose; it's made of relatively hard material, so when combined with other hard surfaces it's likely to make a sharp noise – which could be useful for shocking someone, signalling, or getting or diverting somebody's attention for a brief second.

It has enough structural integrity to use it as a lever of sorts; it is flat enough to put something else on top of for long enough to launch; it gives us a simple rectangular shape complete with templates for drawing or comparing 90 degree angles. If we apply its thin hard edge to something soft with low structural density like a cake, it may suffice as a makeshift knife, or simply it could act as a spacer or a bookmark, maybe even a paperweight or simply a decorative object.

We shouldn't forget that the value of something's performance in a given role depends largely on the context – so it is important to take a holistic view and try to ensure we understand enough about the other elements or factors that the object (in our case, the ruler) may be interacting with. It may be hard and thin enough to cut soft cake which has low structural integrity, but it probably isn't sharp enough to do the same with leather or wood.

This is still a simple ruler we're talking about, but with enough mental application, it can be viewed as an incredibly versatile tool, and I would encourage you to begin to view many other things in a similar way, by exploring their fundamental properties to create some mental hooks as we did with the candle, and then playing with the possibilities that they present regarding similarities or relevant relationships to other situations, items or concepts.

Here's a tip regarding definitions – it applies to hooks in just the same way as it applies to marketing, or any other practice that relies upon meaning, and we've touched upon it in this chapter already. The more detailed you get with your definitions, generally the more finite the applications to which it can be applied. The less detailed you get, the wider a fit you are likely to find, due to there being fewer stated limitations that define what or how this thing is or must be. There are two edges to this metaphorical sword. By becoming less detailed, yes, you widen the possibilities of what fits with that definition, but then you also risk missing some critical factors that might make something specifically relevant (or irrelevant) to the topic in question. Conversely, by getting very detailed in a definition, you risk excluding many possibilities from the looser fringes of things you might associate with it. So, again, ensure you know your context and what you are trying to achieve, in order to understand the level of detail that you will require – and if it's not working, try changing your level of zoom and see if that helps.

If we are applying utilisation to a specific situation, we may want to begin with a wider definition in order to at least be able to generate enough options, and then further qualify them to a suitable shortlist from which we can be confident there is a good solution. And to do that, as we have seen from the chapter on getting things done, it is wise to first define what the actual requirements are:

- What aspects are critical to quality of the output (must haves)?
- What aspects are nice to haves, but not essential (desirables)?
- Any other aspects can be comfortably seen as irrelevant.

I like to call this process of beginning at a wide level of zoom as 'getting all of the toys out', in order to see all the options we've got to play with before we zoom in and qualify where to focus, confirming which options we might want to exclude based upon our must have/ desirable criteria and then seeing what's left (which should be a much smaller set of highly relevant options).

Practising and applying this type of thinking to tools and concepts in your workplace can help you to get much better at finding a good tool for the job or solution to the challenge. And moral and ethical issues aside, it's worth asking if how it gets done is really important if it gets done to an adequate degree. It may not be perfect, but as long as it is good enough, and any moral and legal imperatives are met, then you probably have enough justification to take action and get things done!

Good enough is what happens practically every night and day in theatres and at invitational events around the world. For the organisations putting on a show for their guests, a large part of the experience they deliver revolves around what the audience sees and hears.

Backstage, there is frequently a fervent scurrying, bustle and sometimes outright panic concerned with moving sets, trying to find misplaced props or making last-minute preparations, repairs or fixes, all aimed at producing the professional seamless performance to be experienced at the front of the house.

The audience don't in most cases care about how it happened (again, assuming that this has been achievable within reasonable moral and ethical parameters). All they care about is receiving a smoothly run and enjoyable show. Like the proverbial swan gliding along a lake, on the surface it appears graceful and sublime, but under the water there are feet paddling away like mad. But importantly, thanks to utilisation, the critical to quality elements are delivered.

In applying the principle of utilisation to its fullest, you will realise that it is an incredibly flexible and versatile principle, its use pretty much subject only to the limits of your imagination (didn't I already mention it's useful to expand this?). You may by now be recognising opportunities where utilisation can help you beyond your current workplace – by helping you to improve your chances of finding future workplaces!

By this, I'm talking about the concept of transferrable skills helping you to get future jobs. Transferrable skills (skills or capabilities you possess that can be applied to different situations in several different environments, like the 'meta-skills' I attempt to cover in this book) are a prime example of what utilisation is all about. Recognising what knowledge, skills and abilities you have, understanding their fundamental properties and realising what value these represent to a prospective employer (such as demonstrating that you are able to get a job done) can be an incredibly useful, empowering and uplifting exercise.

Utilisation is one of the core elements of both observational and improvisational comedy, genres which take elements of everyday phenomena and connect them to one another in amusingly unexpected ways. Look at practically any good observational comedy routine and you will find a masterclass in utilisation. But for me, my favourite example of utilisation comes from what is commonly regarded as one of, if not the greatest British comedy duo of all time, Morcambe & Wise. There is an anecdote concerning one particular sketch centred around their bedtime routine; like Bert and Ernie in *Sesame Street*, in the show they were best friends and housemates who, for the purposes of comic effect, also shared a bed. On this occasion, Eric got out of bed to take a look out of the window. At that moment, an ambulance with its sirens wailing passed by. Eric simply turned to look out of the window into the fictional street below, and without hesitating remarked, "He's not going to sell much ice-cream going at that speed, is he?" creating what is for me one of the funniest and most memorable moments in UK comedy TV history. Whether this was (as the legend goes) a genuine ad-lib from the master of the quick-witted one-liner, or an inspired opus from a gifted writer, the final sketch itself is a classic example of how something designed with a very specific purpose (like an ambulance siren), with a little imagination, could be utilised in a totally different way to obtain the desired result. You should be able to find a clip of it online to experience for yourself just how well utilisation served both Eric Morcambe and several generations of grateful viewers.

So, by exercising your imagination, being aware of the power of the tools that you possess (from personal skills and knowledge, to physical resources available to you), and getting good at practising utilisation, you can open an endless world of possibilities and options regarding whatever challenges you may face at work. Through experience you can encounter new situations and recognise elements of them in common with similar situations that you know about, becoming mentally agile enough to create a contingency plan quickly if required – highly desirable skills in today's constantly changing, constantly moving workplace.

The bottom line here? Put simply, I was once asked in an interview what I thought was my strongest skill or talent. My reply was my imagination – because no matter what challenge I faced, even if I had never attempted it before, I knew that I would always be able to imagine what might be a good approach to getting it done, so I would never be at a loss for how to deal with anything that came along. I hope you find it to be as much of a remarkably empowering way of looking at the world as I have.

SUMMARY

- Imagination gives us the power to create possibilities and solutions – and as such is becoming an ever more valued ability over commoditised, repetitive functionality.

- Creating new mental hooks generates more opportunity for connection and insight.

- Practising deeper and more complex observation exercises your ability to find more sophisticated connections in many other areas.

- Messing around and playing with concepts and ideas relaxes our minds, improving our ability to forge new connections.

- Mindfulness can help us to find innovative ways around logical problems.

- Utilisation can free up our perceptual limitations and reveal solutions that are right in front of us.

- The larger and less detailed the chunk, the higher the chance of finding similarity. The smaller and more detailed the chunk, the higher the chance of finding difference.

CHAPTER 7
EFFECTIVE LEARNING

This chapter will help you to understand how learning happens in terms of some of the processes occurring in your mind, the stages of learning through which we move, and how to make learning happen more effectively for you.

KNOWLEDGE & LEARNING: A SYMBIOTIC RELATIONSHIP

Before we go into detail on the process, I would like to explore the concepts of learning and knowledge. Why? Because understanding their relationship will shed light on the importance of continuing to learn throughout your career (and indeed life), recognising that learning is not just something that we should do at the start of our lives and then complete, but an ongoing journey, which, if we allow, can keep our lives full of excitement and freshness, maintaining our zeal to live and enjoy as well as giving us the self-confidence to know that whatever comes our way, we are well equipped to be able to adapt to it.

THE TAO OF WORK FU

"Change is the end result of all true learning."

Leo Buscaglia PhD[32]

Learning is the process of exploring, recognising and gaining new insight, and if we so wish, of taking that insight and being able to achieve something new, whether it be a new skill, a new level of performance or simply new understandings and ways of looking at the world. But in order to learn, we must feed the process with new knowledge. Knowledge is the fuel, if you will, that enables learning to happen and continue. Sometimes we accumulate new knowledge from reading or observing. Sometimes others share their knowledge with us, and sometimes we generate it in the form of new insights, gained by reflecting on experiences, the effects of actions we have taken, or combining existing knowledge bundles we may have in new ways. By generating new knowledge we enable the possibility for us to gain further insight. If we stop feeding the process with new knowledge, there is a danger that our learning will slow down and we run the risk of our environment overtaking us leading to us becoming contextually obsolete, as was the fate that befell the sabre-toothed tiger. So learning allows us to exert some degree of control in being able to change our environment, ourselves and our destiny.

Equally, knowledge on its own is just information, data, with no or little meaning. Data and statistics on their own aren't important – it's the relationships between them and their contexts that count. The power of information lies in the way in which we use it and understand its meaning in a given context. Making this leap of recognition requires learning to take place, and in turn learning can give us new insights into the utility of information that we thought we knew, helping us make the step from merely having knowledge to possessing wisdom.

So it's clear, learning and knowledge are highly interdependent on one another; to learn, we need a constant supply of knowledge, and when we get it and are able to learn, we are also able to generate new knowledge which itself further enriches the learning process. It's a virtuous circle, and one that continually feeds my personal curiosity for life – not only in understanding more about life, but also in firing up the possibilities of how I (and others) could use that new understanding.

So, now that we understand the relationship between knowledge (the fuel) and learning (the process that synthesises it into meaningful and practical tools) let's look at the continuum along which we move when learning a new skill.

THE LEARNING PROCESS

Commonly referred to as the Conscious Competence learning model, I occasionally also term this the 'Rumsfeld Continuum', in reference to Donald Rumsfeld's speech during the Gulf War in which he attempted to describe to the world's press the several states of understanding about a situation that the US had acknowledged it had either attained or was facing. While it may receive its share of satirical commentary, the gist of what Mr. Rumsfeld was trying to say is embedded within the learning process everyone undergoes when facing any new situation. Here's the transcript as he said it:

"Reports that say that something hasn't happened are always interesting to me, because as we know, there are known knowns; there are things that we know that we know. We also know there are known unknowns; that is to say we know there are some things we do not know. But there are also unknown unknowns, the ones we don't know we don't know." [33]

In effect he was describing, in a roundabout way, several of the different stages of learning (or in this specific case understanding) that the US faced after its decision to go to war in the Middle East. This awareness, that in addition to what the US did know, there were things that they acknowledged still needed to be discovered is the basic first step towards greater understanding, learning and progress, and thus a solid platform from where to begin. For the purposes of this chapter (indeed much of this book), this awareness of the need for learning (or change) signals the start of the learning journey – the one that takes us from unawareness to awareness, to concentration, to naturalisation, so I shall now elaborate on the stages of the model itself.

- *Unconscious Incompetence* (unawareness) – not knowing what you don't know. This is an extremely difficult stage to be at, as it is the one where it is most likely that you can make large mistakes because you are totally unaware of the criteria or knowledge required to make any relevant progress. Breaking through this stage is perhaps going to help you make the most progress in your pursuit of that which you are trying to learn, as without it, no progress can be made at all as there is no idea of where to focus or what to learn. Zooming further out, this stage can also describe the state in which we do not even know that learning or progress is required, and therefore make no effort to even find out what might be an objective to strive towards.

- *Conscious Incompetence* (awareness of the general requirements) – being aware of what you do not know, and as a result having a good idea of the things that you now need to know more about. Getting to this stage represents a big step forward, as you should now at least be aware of what you don't know, and as a result can more easily direct your efforts to do something about it! Getting through this stage means finding out about the general directions and topics that you need to follow and learn more about, so you will not simply be trying to take on the world and learn everything there is to know in the hope that by random chance you will have covered the exact areas of knowledge that you need right now. Each time you gain new insight, you have a new area on which to focus, and can begin to build a picture of all of the elements and subject areas that you will be required to learn about. This stage is about enabling you to choose where to focus your efforts. As individuals, we do not have infinite time and resource to hope and wait for random chance to help us out – so being able to focus is of huge importance to our making progress.

- *Conscious Competence* (focused deliberate practice in those areas that you know are required) – with some focused effort and attention you should now be able to perform an activity that you are learning to some degree of competence. You may even get to the stage where you can perform it to a good degree consistently, though this will take focused effort and practice.

CHAPTER 7: EFFECTIVE LEARNING

- *Unconscious Competence* (naturalisation of the action) – Congratulations! If you have persevered and reached this stage, you will have learnt to perform the desired activity as if it was second nature – you will no longer need to concentrate hard on doing so, as it has become akin to habit. What's actually happened is that the memory of all the elements required for you to perform the activity have been embedded in a part of your brain called the basal ganglia, making them automatic and requiring much less mental effort for you to be able to perform them to an adequate degree. There are many examples that we could use to see this process in action: driving is a typical one, making a cup of tea or coffee or getting our breakfast ready, and while most of us cannot remember the early days of learning to walk, and so cannot compare, anyone who has had a broken leg will remember that strange and at times frustrating process of retraining the muscles to walk once it has been released from the cast.

This last example tends to stick in the mind of anyone who has endured it, as it is an example of when we have learnt something to that automatic level, but then had our 'expertise' (in this case, actually our muscle memory) reduced to a lower level of competence in the continuum. Regardless of whether you're now a highly competent driver, or have broken your leg, there are still many examples around us every day that illustrate this process nicely: watching toddlers trying to take their first steps, a child practising how to write legibly, or in fact anyone trying out a new activity for the first few times (golf, ice skating, bowling – physical activities lend themselves well to helping us remember this feeling) all allow us to either feel or observe how much concentration is required at the beginning of the learning process.

There is debate that there is in fact a fifth stage in the learning process which is required in order to be able to teach what we know to others effectively. For those who have acquired some degree of unconscious competence, it is widely considered that this stage often requires us to take a step back from the automatic level of competence we have accrued. Doing so allows us to analyse and deconstruct what is actually happening in our performance so that we may be able to describe it to others, and come up with ways by which they can both more easily understand what we are talking about, and find structured ways by which they can apply relevant practice to get better at it. I would support this school of thought, as from having done so myself on several occasions, I believe that in reassessing the components of the skill or activity that we often carry out without thought, we are able to focus on exactly what is happening and how, and synthesise a new version that allows us to improve. Laying out the steps can also allow others to grasp, learn or improve quickly some aspect of it themselves.

By stepping outside of the process in this way, we are able to view it from two different viewpoints: reflecting on both the steps that we went through and our feelings and first-hand experience of its dynamic. This can give a third party insight not just into what to do, but also what to expect in terms of how it might make them feel (not quite full experiential preparation, but at least helping them to reduce surprise somewhat through awareness). And I would also argue that this stage is not necessarily confined to someone who has achieved some degree of competence or mastery in performing the subject themselves. Some may not need to take a step back, but can guide and teach others due to their conscious understanding of a subject. José Mourinho was never a footballer but has proven himself to be excellent at coaching footballers how to play effectively; most male obstetricians have never been pregnant (at least this is the prevalent state of healthcare science at the time of publishing) but are usually effective at being able to advise women on their natal journey.

In fact, regardless of whether you intend to teach or share your learnings with others or not, I would suggest that by incorporating this stage into your regular learning process (and many people already do) you can greatly enhance it. As we shall shortly explore, reflection offers us the chance to build an objective feedback loop through which we can deconstruct, analyse and better understand what happened in a given situation, so that like Team GB Cycling we might be able to synthesise or at least visualise a new improved method that we can use in our next practice efforts. If you are concerned that you don't know how to do this yet, don't worry, there is still hope; this is exactly what coaching is for, where someone else is able to take time and an objective view to help you find ways in which you might be able to make improvements. Good coaches should also be able to help you develop the skills to do it for yourself on an ongoing basis. How long you spend in each stage will vary and is subject to many factors, including:

- Your propensity to learn. Whether this has been influenced by your genetics, having developed a learning mindset that is primed and ready to learn, or simply the context of the subject we are trying to learn (subjects we enjoy typically are easier to learn about – at least as long as we continue to enjoy them), we all have different abilities in this respect, with some of us being able to learn certain things more easily than others at certain times.

- The learning method(s) being used.

- Complexity of the task/breadth of the field of knowledge required to be understood. This itself can be influenced by the scope of the area you have chosen to become competent in. Setting your next learning milestone as being able to play the next new guitar chord is likely to increase your chances of success over attempting to learn how to play an entire song which may contain many chords, several of which may be new, as will the combinations of chords in order for the music to flow. As we saw in the chapter on getting things done, breaking things down can have a huge impact on helping us to maintain progress over a period of time in learning, just as much as in any other project.

- The amount of time you practise for and frequency of your sessions. It has become generally accepted that we are not robots, so practising something for every hour of our waking lives is for almost all of us out of the question, even if we didn't have pressing matters like keeping the rest of our lives going to deal with. We also have a limited amount of cognitive attention before we need a rest (typically through sleep). According to sports writer, broadcaster and Olympian Matthew Sayed, even elite performers can only really focus for around three hours maximum per session before the return on learning effort invested seriously declines.[34] On some work we may have to keep going to meet a deadline, but when it comes to learning, if we use a last-minute massive cram technique on a regular basis, much of our effort will be to little effect when compared to a longer cycle that employs more regular, smaller efforts.

- The gap between your starting level of competence in the required skill or area of knowledge and the level you aim to get to. As with setting milestones and smaller, more frequent goals, we can adjust the way in which we manage the size of each chunk of learning to give ourselves a psychological boost in being able to see progression, rather than having one big far away goal that until it is all complete remains 'unaccomplished' on any checklist.

The Good News About Learning

Many of these have an influence over the effectiveness of your practice and how well or quickly you pick up a new skill or body of knowledge. While I'm not going to go into much further exploration of the differences in our propensity to learn, genetically or otherwise, I would, however, like to highlight the fact that neuroscience has shown that no matter how old we get, our brains have the capacity to rewire themselves continually in order for us to keep learning throughout our lives. This is called brain plasticity, and for me is an incredibly exciting and uplifting piece of research, as it reinforces one of the basic motivational criteria that we all need in order to take the early steps and continue our efforts in striving to achieve anything: hope.

Reflection – A Critical Advantage

An interesting thing to note about our evolution is that we also have the capacity to reflect consciously on our situations. Douglas Hofstadter remarks that this is one of the key things that enable us to have a notion of being a person, rather than just another animal – we define ourselves by being able to notice and observe ourselves.[35] He calls this a 'feedback loop' – the ability to step out of the immediate moment and observe and analyse what we are doing and the situations that we are in. This could be described as 'meta-thinking'– or consideration of things beyond the immediate direct sensations that we experience as creatures (for instance, concepts beyond our immediate geography, physical presence and even timeframe). This is a very important concept to understand if we are to develop, as it allows us to think not just about the immediate situation, but also the possible wider consequences of that situation, and even think about the way that our thought process is happening (thinking about how we are thinking), enabling us, if we choose, to make adjustments to try and improve the immediate or possible future situations in our favour. This has given us a huge evolutionary advantage over other animals, and only serves to continually increase the effectiveness and the rate at which we are able to learn. We have become capable of self-improvement, rather than just waiting and hoping that natural evolution or the effect of chaos theory gives us a lucky break.

The Joy Of The Steep Learning Curve

So let's look at some perceptions that can affect our learning. Remember, this is meant as an introduction, so you may want to explore some of them in greater detail in your own time, but I hope it will at least advance you through the early stages of any learning curve you encounter by helping you to find a solid 'why' to spark your motivation on your objectives, and in showing you what to expect, also removing some of the anxiety and fear of the unknown that can drain momentum, enabling you to keep at it until you reach some stage of competence that can show you your efforts are paying off.

Much of the bulk of what we need to learn comes at the start of the learning process (in fact much of it involves learning where we need to focus, or in effect, cutting out the majority of stuff that we could possibly learn but don't need to). But the phrase 'steep learning curve' is often greeted with a wince, as people often think that this means an activity is difficult to learn; a steep curve actually indicates that much progress can be made in a short period of time. The feeling of anxiety associated with steep learning curves probably refers to the fact that in learning we will make mistakes due to our lack of understanding, and making mistakes is generally regarded as a bad thing. This is something that we could do with changing our attitude towards.

"Would you like me to give you a formula for success? It's quite simple, really. Double your rate of failure."

Thomas J. Watson, founder of IBM

This quote is true in the sense that our goal is not to fail more times, but to speed up the rate at which we take action in an attempt to meet our goals. By the nature of the learning curve, there will be more mistakes and things that we don't get right at the start, so as long as with each we are taking some time to understand why the previous attempt did not work and adjusting our next effort, then the consequence will be that we power through these elementary mistakes and increase our level of competence that much more quickly.

Josh Kaufman suggests that the biggest barrier to learning is an emotional one.[36] As we saw in the chapters on change and getting things done, the uncomfortable feelings of failure or inadequacy that we associate with mistakes can often be a strong reason for us to avoid even beginning in the first place. We must therefore prepare ourselves to acknowledge getting things wrong as a natural part of the process, otherwise we will give up (or not even begin) in the face of accumulated (or even just perceived potential) demoralisation.

Some of the more enlightened teachers and mentors I have encountered encourage mistakes in new learning ventures, and I feel they (both the mentors and the mistakes) should be celebrated (just a little, of course) for several reasons:

- It shows that the student has been brave enough to make an attempt at the task in question.

- There is almost always some opportunity to learn something new from taking action in any given situation.

- Encouraging the student to embrace the fact that making mistakes is an entirely natural part of the learning process helps to reduce the personal aspect of failure and encourage the student to keep going.

It's Not An Ego Trip

I find that practising humility can be a very useful tool in this instance – letting go of our pride and accepting that mistakes will happen, and are supposed to happen more frequently in this period. Our egos are the things that try to protect us from situations where we feel others may be judging us and finding us lacking. It happens everywhere, from the workplace to social and leisure pursuits. I often find this when going to the gym after some absence. I should begin on light weights and ease myself back in so as to allow my muscles to accustom themselves to the new rigour and be suitably conditioned to manage heavier weights, reducing the risk of injury from trying to lift too heavily too quickly. But watching people in there who are already into their heavy lifting regimes (and who are in many cases a good deal larger and stronger than I am anyway), I sometimes feel a need to show my mettle and demonstrate that while I may not be able to match them in terms of total weight, I can impress with the amount of weight someone of my size can handle. This type of ego-led thinking results in either avoidance of the gym (flight from the threat of social inadequacy) or me injuring myself as I try to go too heavy too soon (which is the result of me trying to 'fight' the feelings generated by what I think are other people's perceptions of me). Recognising that this is happening helps me to reassess my feelings and reappraise the situation; I am able to remind myself that most of the people in the gym have been there in the same situation, and probably have had (or are also currently having) the same feelings, which are nothing more than perceptions based upon assumption. Also knowing the vast number of different fitness and health-related goals that people can set from their gym time, plus the fact that everyone should ideally follow a regime that is tailored to their own goals and capabilities, and it becomes a lot easier for me to put aside my pride and start on the very light weights. The natural reaction doesn't disappear, but in being aware of what internal process is occurring, I improve my chance of being able to manage it.

What The Learning Curve Means

In addition to reinforcing our resilience to the woes of repeated early mistakes, a steep learning curve has other not so obvious benefits if we decide to get on board for the ride.

It acts as a barrier to entry that prevents many people from being regarded as competent in many skills or fields simply because of their fear of it and the ego sting of inevitable initial failures. Having the bravery to step out of our comfort zone and accepting the pain of the early stages of the learning curve can allow us to rise quickly above the normal skill level of those who do not persist and give up after a few early setbacks – or who did not even dare to try. If you commit to putting in a concerted effort you will find you can amass a highly useful set of skills relatively quickly. In a world in which it is getting increasingly more difficult to stand out and differentiate ourselves, marrying this understanding to the knowledge of what to expect through the typical learning process can give us a strong reason to keep going and remove enough anxiety to allow us to feel more confident about exploring new areas in which we can learn and self-improve, safe in the knowledge that advancing our capabilities (and the world's perception of them) is eminently achievable with a little effort.

In *The First 20 Hours* Kaufman establishes a theory that a degree of competence in most skills can be attained with – you guessed it – just 20 hours of focused, deliberate practice. In order to get the most out of these 20 hours, one must separate the initial learning required into individual areas on which to focus, identifying the most important aspects of a subject or skill – a big step in helping ourselves to move past the unconscious incompetence stage. You can then devote attention to practising them effectively and reinforcing your momentum by providing frequent points at which you can recognise your progress and feel a sense of effectiveness about your overall efforts. It also reduces the threat level of each new piece of learning, reducing the chance that we will avoid doing it by running away from it or procrastinating.

Whether the learning curve for our particular objective is a lot longer than a single skill (e.g. becoming a brain surgeon versus learning how to ride a bike), or is small enough for us to become unconsciously competent in less than the arbitrarily prescribed 20 hours, you are both free to continue your journey to new levels of performance or incorporate new, perhaps complementary areas of skill or knowledge, buoyed by the fact that you have progressed a lot in a short space of time and now know that you have a good understanding of the process to be able to do so again.

After a certain point, there is of course a diminishing rate of return on the effort we are investing, and we may decide that adding the further levels of expertise or mastery will not be worth it to us. We don't all have the goal of winning the gold medal or being one of the elite where the 10,000 hours are required to gain the finest of extra margins that complete mastery requires. But for most skills, by simple, focused application we can quickly position ourselves a good way beyond many of those around us who have not attempted to do so in this particular area, and thus be considered more competent or more of an expert than they are – a handy position to be in when competing for jobs or business. This has interesting consequences in the workplace, as frequently we simply do not have time to study any specific area to the point of becoming an elite level expert, but looking at both Kaufman's research and learning curves, it appears that we do not necessarily need to do so in order to become effective enough to be seen as competent, positively differentiated and of value to our organisation.

WHAT IS YOUR LEARNING GOAL?

So now you should be more aware of what to expect and the stages of competence that you will pass through whenever you decide to improve your knowledge or skills in any way. Importantly, you will also have a good idea of what must be done in the crucial early stages i.e. researching and establishing the important areas of knowledge or skill that you must learn in order to make the progress you want. But you can further improve the speed and return on your efforts by defining the types of learning activities that would be most effective. If you were learning to juggle, all the reading in the world won't help you to develop the necessary motor skills and coordination that would be required to perform such a task. And conversely, starting off practising with chainsaws and flaming batons (because that's how the guy you saw on the TV does it) is likely to slow your progress somewhat. In essence, by exploring how might be the best ways to learn what you need to learn, you can provide yourself with more clarity and detail on the exact nature of the tasks required. To make this easier, you can use a reference structure called Bloom's Taxonomy.[37]

The committee that developed it (chaired by Benjamin Bloom after whom the Taxonomy was named) had the aim of developing a breakdown of different levels of learning and classifying them into understandable groups or 'domains' which related to the type of learning. There were three domains: cognitive, which focused on development of knowledge, comprehension and critical thinking; affective concerned emotional reactions, attitudes and feelings; and psychomotor which concerned itself with physical skills. As the purpose of this book is primarily to equip you with a greater understanding of workplace dynamics and your role in them, I will focus on the cognitive domain. Beginning at simply being able to remember something regardless of our understanding of it in any way, the different learning levels of the cognitive domain (which have been developed since the original taxonomy was published) are now held as being:

- *Remember* – simply being able to remember a list of words in rote fashion without actually understanding anything more about them other than being able to repeat them when asked.

- *Understand* – often referred to in reading terms as comprehension, this is the difference between simply being aware that something exists (being able to remember it) and actually knowing something about it – do you need to be able to organise or summarise the information you know?

- *Apply* – Do you need to use knowledge you have to solve problems in new areas, or to find different ways of solving existing challenges?

- *Analyse* – Do you need to be able to examine the relationships, principles and dynamics between elements of information and draw conclusions from that analysis?

- *Evaluate* – Will you want to be able to make and defend judgments about the validity of information, ideas or the quality of output, based upon given criteria?

- *Synthesise/Create* – Will you need to combine the knowledge you have into a new structure, output or abstract concept?

The earlier levels of the taxonomy are known as lower order thinking where individual pieces of information or knowledge about them are seen as being largely separate and isolated in their own right, while the higher a level we strive for, the more the requirement that we utilise more nuanced relationships between the pieces of information we have in more complex, sophisticated and often abstract ways.

We can see then that different sets of cognitive skills will be required for each stage, and in order for this to happen, different combinations of learning practices will be required for us to develop those skills.

For example, simply learning to remember a list of items may only require that we practise repeatedly implanting those pieces of information into our minds until we are able to remember them, without any need to understand anything about them. No relationships, effect or contextual value they may have in relation to anything else other than their name.

But processing many pieces of information and their relationships to given contexts that enable us to make and justify decisions will require a whole other set of cognitive skills, and we would need to practise developing these in several different ways in order to get a grip fully on how to utilise them effectively.

In exploring how some people are able to produce exceptional levels of performance, Matthew Sayed explains that to reach elite performance levels in table tennis requires understanding and instant evaluation, processing and reaction to countless contextual cues that enable a lighting fast winning response.[38] I would suggest that while this example focuses primarily on the motor skill domain, there is a principle here that we can apply to the cognitive domain, and that is the principle of context. In the workplace, there are far fewer limits as to the scope, variety and complexity of the contexts we could face than in a game of table tennis – quite scary. This does not bode well for our chances of responding with an appropriate way that is of benefit to us.

Fortunately for most of us, we are not usually living on the edge of elite level performance in every minute of every day at work; the workplace is a lot more forgiving in several ways. It is rare that we have to respond with a lightning fast reaction that instantly decides whether we win or lose; even in pressure situations, we have much more time in which to evaluate and choose our response. Secondly, there is less of a fine line between instantly winning and losing. There is a much wider scope for our actions to fall into the 'good enough' category, plus more opportunities for future actions to influence our chances of success. Finally, work is not always a win/lose competition. Despite the sometimes dog-eat-dog portrayal of some workplaces in fictional media, it is frequently more flexible in terms of colleagues and customers being prepared to accept an occasional slight dip in performance, as long as they feel that their concerns are being addressed and that the dip is likely to be a temporary thing. Nevertheless, the principle of being able to understand and evaluate the unique contextual dynamics of situations in which a large number of factors may or may not have an influence, and make a justifiable decision based on this evaluation, is still a highly valuable ability. It is something that many organisations would like their staff to either possess or develop, as it means good decision making can be trusted to individual level employees, as opposed to older, yet still prevalent more centralised decision-making models where managers must approve decisions, slowing things down and increasing the cost of doing so. This is the result of low trust – where more junior staff are not trusted to be capable of making decisions resulting in a higher cost to the organisation.

Like any project, defining the desired outcome of a learning journey helps us to make decisions about the 'how' – what we need to do to achieve it. Bloom's Taxonomy can therefore be a useful reference map to guide you in deciding what your learning goals are, what they need not be, and as a result, which would be the most effective and expedient learning methods you may need to employ.

A Practical Approach To Learning

So we now have a useful template for planning any learning path by plotting out:

Being aware of a need to learn something and thus knowing why it must happen.

Getting an understanding of the degree (or level) of learning that we will need to achieve our objectives (answering the need). Identifying what the most important skills/learnings we will need to become proficient. With these established, you can now begin to plan your Work Breakdown Structure that will list the actual tasks you need to carry out. These will include what type of learning activities you will need to include, and what preparation you will need to do to allow you to focus on them. Here are some different types of learning methods you may want to employ.

Theory

- Uses – This is useful for those early stages when we need to get a feel for what exactly we need to be focusing on at a general level. What are the most important areas on which to focus? Theory gives us structures and frameworks and some degree of conceptual dynamics.

- Theoretical learning is somewhat limited, as on its own it is a very static method of learning. By this I mean that students can only learn what information has been provided to them or what is covered in the theory, and as theories typically require a substantial amount of work and time to develop and test, learning anything beyond what is contained in the theory is not really possible or fluid without other learning practices. Frameworks can also fall foul of being relevant to a specific situation. What happens if we face variants on these? Real life has a habit of throwing multiple, complex and often dynamic variables at us on any given subject.

Observation

- Observing examples of the subject to be learnt in action can add depth to our understanding of theory, by allowing us to see several different aspects of that theory being put to use in real situations which can vary from the exact theoretical model. It allows us to see a few more of the dynamic nuances required for execution, and can also validate elements of the theory in our minds, giving us more confidence in it.

- However, like theory, observation on its own is somewhat limited in that it can usually only provide learning within the boundaries of examples provided, and is influenced by the interpretation of the example by the observer. By simply observing, a learner cannot fully understand all of the internal processes and feelings that the person involved in the example may have been experiencing.

Social Learning/Interaction

- Social learning is an extremely valuable method of learning as it promotes the sharing of knowledge, opinion and evaluation of its validity on a wider scale than we could ever experience on our own. By sharing our thoughts with others and allowing them to share their thoughts and feedback with us, we are able to increase the variety of cognitive input that we and the group receive and can consider, leading to a higher chance that some of those thoughts will allow us to make significant leaps of understanding, and produce new and useful insights. This is why communication is so important. The interactive aspect of social learning means that we can vastly increase the rate of exploration and validation of our learning – and even if that means there will be a higher number of failures, it also means that as a group, there is also likely to be a higher number of successes.

- Examples of the power of social learning can be found in situations when you are at a loss for what to do, or you believe that you are facing a decision that is definitely outside of your official authority or experience to make. An option in these situations could be to ask your manager for guidance and feedback as to the decisions you think you should make. (Always have your 'why' handy for these!) It is after all a large part of what they are there for – to enable their staff and others to help the company to progress. Ideally, you should not just be asking them to make the decision, but proposing possible solutions to them and asking them to explain how they evaluated and made that decision, so that perhaps you can learn how better to do so next time. While some managers may see this as trying to encroach on their territory and get defensive, many will recognise the benefits of investing in their staff, not least of which being the opportunity to free up some of their time, allowing them to focus on activities which can add even more value to the

- company. It also helps you to learn and progress, giving them a stronger team, and improving the chances that you will all produce successful results.

- While social learning allows us to share much more information and explore many more specific targeted elements of what we are trying to learn very quickly, again, social learning can only give us so much insight into the full learning experience because we are still relying on conveyance of information in other people's terminologies, and as we have seen in the chapter on communication, we each have our own map of the world. Our communication with others is also highly selective, as thanks to phenomena such as the curse of knowledge, there is a myriad of information that we don't communicate to others as we assume much of it is commonly understood and doesn't need communicating.

Experiential (Learning By Doing)

- Taking action in an attempt to achieve a goal is one of the best methods to understand a given skill in a real life environment. The big difference between practice and any of the other learning types is that it allows you to experience the effects of the myriad number of often random or unforeseen variables that real life can throw at you. Because you are experiencing it first hand, it usually engages you more than any of the other methods. This combination – deeper engagement and the challenge of dealing with such a wide number of sometimes fluctuating variables – allows you to learn at a much faster rate.

- Being 'in the moment' can be great for rapid learning and performance improvement in a particular area of focus. But there are some dangers that come from taking it to the extreme. We may limit our development if we only ever focus on repeating the same actions over and over and never seek alternative ways to amend and improve our practice. Too intense a focus for too long can sometimes blinker our understanding of the wider picture: other possibilities or factors beyond this immediate point of focus that it may be helpful to consider. And of course it is essential that we make sure we are practising the right things in the right way as repeated practice of the wrong thing is not only a waste of time, but could result in us getting very good at doing something incorrectly.

Reflection

- Reflection after performing a task is hugely complementary to practical application in improving how effective we are at learning. Questions such as asking oneself whether or not the goal was achieved, what went well, what didn't go well, and how things could be done differently all provide opportunity for course correction – small improvements in each iteration that can improve the effectiveness of the overall process, whether that is in actual practical application or simply understanding of it. Effectively it is taking some time out of the direct activity to ascertain what is working and what can be improved.

- Reflection can provide insight – but like theory, these insights must be tried out and tested (by another round of practical application) in order to understand their real dynamics or give some weight to their validity.

By obtaining some understanding of the useful dynamics and potential limitations of each method of learning, I hope you can see that it is rare that one on its own will do the job if a significant level of learning in Bloom's Taxonomy is the goal. As we can see with the often quite narrowly defined scope of knowledge that theory can provide, the opportunity for wider and more varied knowledge capture that social learning presents, and the highly complementary relationship that exists between practical application and reflection (which is in effect creation of new adjusted theory that through further application can also be tested and refined), it is fairly obvious that a combination of each of these which utilises their strengths as per the context of our learning requirements is going to deliver a much more effective and efficient learning experience. Combining methods in this way is referred to as 'blended learning'.

Keeping Your Hard-Earned Knowledge

When we see, hear or experience something for the first time, some of that experience may stay with us in our memory. This is the whole point of training courses. Demonstrate something new to the learners so that they may be able to learn and acquire the new skill, knowledge or competence and repeat or utilise it in the future – the sharing and passing on of understanding and capability. What is not always understood about learning, however, is that it doesn't readily happen as the result of one isolated learning effort.

The Forgetting Curve

Some of the knowledge we are exposed to gets stored in an area of our brain called the basal ganglia, where it is believed our long-term memory resides and from where it can be recalled for future use. But not much of this happens on first encounter with the information. The rest of the knowledge is still floating around the transient tiny stage of the prefrontal cortex as the next of the millions of pieces of information continually flying around us vies for priority in our thinking. As a result, the amount of the original knowledge that we are able to retain decays quickly, with less and less retained the further away from the original learning effort we get.

This principle is referred to as the 'forgetting curve', and is based upon research carried out by Herman Ebbinghaus who tested his recall of a series of lists of words over a period of time in order to better understand how well our memories can retain information. Recall of a list without any need to know more about the items, properties or dynamics in a given situation is one of the simpler levels of cognitive learning in Bloom's Taxonomy, and though conducted over 100 years ago, his findings have stood the test of time and indicated that:

- Within 20 minutes 42% of the memorised list was lost.

- Within 24 hours 67% of what he learnt had vanished.

- After a month 79% had been forgotten, meaning just 21% of what was learnt was remembered.

These results have come to be acknowledged as a typical benchmark measurement for knowledge retention, and illustrate a quite shocking rate of decay, to the point where they almost make you really question the amount of effort it might take to learn something if the retention rate is so low. The good news is that this was not the end of Ebbinghaus's research and represented the rate of decay without any follow-up to the original learning he conducted.

What he also found was that spaced repetition was one of the best ways to help either delay or reduce the rate at which the lists were forgotten, and improve the amount of learnt information that was retained and embedded in long-term memory.[39]

Repetition

There have been further studies into the effect of repetition that have cascaded down through our work environments. The resulting insights have suggested that repetition acts on several levels to help us remember information, including:

- Making the information more familiar to us, and therefore less new and less of a threat – making it OK for us to move towards and embrace it rather than rejecting (moving away from) it.

- Repetition creates a pattern. Our brains like patterns – they provide consistency to help us make sense of our world, so we are naturally primed to notice them.

- Repetition gives us several attempts to make new neural connections between the new knowledge and knowledge we already possess – reinforcing the chances of us being able to recall it.

CHAPTER 7: EFFECTIVE LEARNING

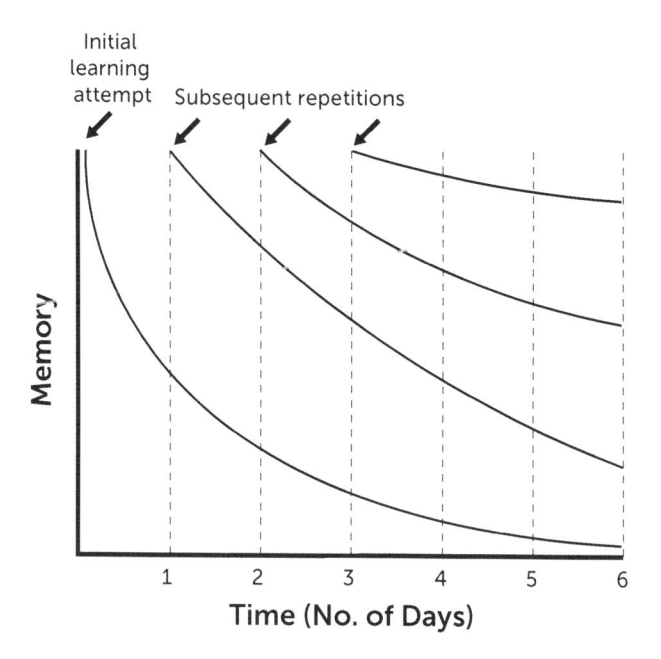

Representation of Ebbinghaus's Forgetting Curve and the Effects of Spaced Repetition on Knowledge Retention

This emphasis on repetition as a critical way to help people remember things has had quite an effect throughout the world – driving the popularity of media advertising and resulting in a mantra commonly put to such uses as advising students writing essays right through to coaching executives making corporate presentations: begin by briefly telling your audience what you are going to tell them, tell them about it in a bit more detail, then briefly summarise what you have just told them again at the end.

As with other learning tools, repetition on its own isn't going to help you develop the understanding you need to learn something in the first place, but it can help you to better retain and be able to recall the information that you have learnt at some point in the future, if required. So whenever you go on a course or receive any kind of training, if you aren't given the chance to do so during the course itself, look to practise it a few times the same day – simply by trying to summarise or explain to yourself or others what you have learnt so far. In fact, the more different ways you can use to do so, the wider the range of different neural networks you will utilise, and as per the principles of blended learning and the forgetting curve, the greater the chances of you being able to recall it at a later date. Then commit to do more repetition the very next day by explaining it again, discussing it more, or if possible actually doing it and applying your learning to a real situation. This will help to embed more of what you have taken in and reduce the chances that it will evaporate, never to be seen again. I might even be so bold as to suggest that you do just that with some of the topics or points from this book. I believe you'll thank me for it, at least I hope you'll remember to!

The Power of Analogy

I round off this chapter with a section devoted to a concept which, though at its core is a very useful communication tool, via utilisation also lends itself nicely to helping you to be able to learn more effectively, and improves your ability to help others more easily take in and learn what you have to share.

What we learn (and remember) depends largely upon us being able to make reference to something we already understand or know – an efficient way of growing and enriching our perceptual map of the world and how it works. Analogy has long been hailed as a highly effective way of communicating many, sometimes complex ideas simply in a shape or format that our audience can easily understand. As we can see with phrases like "When angry, he was the devil himself" or "She leapt like a salmon to intercept the ball", metaphors and similes, ways of describing things in abstract terms that offer a common level of understanding often of purely conceptual ideas (such as principles), are in fact analogies.

Pulitzer prize-winning author and Professor of Cognitive Science Douglas Hofstadter proposes that analogy lies at the core of cognition, and as alluded to in the chapter on imagination, suggests that all of the concepts that we understand are merely bundles of interlinked stories about everything we have perceived in the world (our personal perception maps) that we have already built. In thinking, he suggests that we are simply moving fluidly from concept to concept, and that the connections between the bundles are the similarities between analogies that each bundle shares. This concept itself, he suggests, may explain why experience makes it easier to organise and digest new learning.[40] By creating an abstract representation of something, we are in most cases encouraging the audience (or ourselves) to make reference to only some of its more obvious properties – in effect, simplifying it for each effort, and making it easier for us to mentally manipulate it. The analogies are like boxes, holding much detail, but presenting an easily useable form.

The saying "A picture paints a thousand words" could also be validated in this light if we consider that words are simply symbolic representations of very small pieces of meaning, requiring a lot of attention and focus to decode, and translate each one both individually and within its context. In this manner, I see analogy as a form of chunking up, thereby increasing the chances that similarities will be found with whatever idea I am trying to explain or convey. And by increasing the chances of finding points of similarity, we are increasing the chances of our audience remembering them, as they will suddenly seem a whole lot more familiar, meaning we can enjoy the benefits that repetition brings to the process of knowledge retention. Given that it is estimated over 50% of our brain is related to processing visual information, this might explain the increase in popularity of video and infographic formats to convey information in both workplace and learning environments. Receiving information in a visual format could be a very efficient and effective way to help us focus and remember, as it would logically suggest that we were playing to its strengths and reducing the amount of effort spent on other types of information reprocessing activities.

For more evidence as to the power of analogy, consider a common technique used by memory experts the world over. While it doesn't necessarily give them any insight into the information, it does help them to retain it effectively. They create what are called 'memory palaces' which allow them to pull off feats such as being able to remember the exact order of 20 decks of shuffled cards after only an hour's study; but at its core, this technique is also useful for such everyday matters as merely remembering the names of people you have just met. It works on the principle of association (a core principle of analogy) where the exponent creates an imaginary journey through a palace they have mentally created. On their journey they place a pictorial representation of each thing they need to remember. Each element is associated with a highly memorable object, usually the more outrageous the better, so a big person from Newcastle might be remembered as a huge bottle of Newcastle Brown Ale; if they had a vibrant personality the bottle might have been shaken up and be fizzing over. By associating the things they want to remember with vivid images in a flamboyant story, they are in effect creating a chain of mental hooks which are easier to remember as:

1. They are using a visual format.

2. On account of their ostentatious and colourful nature, the stories and elements in them are extremely different from the norms of most of our everyday lives, and as we know, our brains are wired to be able to detect difference effectively.

SUMMARY

- Learning is enriched by new knowledge. New knowledge is generated by learning. One feeds the other.

- When learning we move though a continuum from being unaware to being unconsciously competent.

- Becoming good enough at something is wholly more achievable than striving for elite level performance.

- We have the ability to keep learning throughout our lives; reflection is a key tool in helping us make more sense of what has happened or experiences we have had.

- Learning by doing is an incredibly rich and effective method of learning.

- Steep learning curves are an opportunity for rapid progress.

- Making mistakes in our early attempts is a normal part of the learning process – and a good indicator of our potential for progress (as long as it's not the same mistake each time).

- We should choose our learning methods to fit our learning objectives.

- Repetition and practice are vital to helping us remember what we have learnt over the longer term.

- Analogy can help make it easier for our brains to remember information in the first place by connecting it to something we already know.

CHAPTER 8

THE BEDROCK OF SELLING

The subject of sales is for me a very interesting one. This is partly because of the fine line between being perceived as either a trusted partner or a seedy operator looking to profit at someone else's expense, but also because like many of the other areas this book explores, it is so pervasive in practically every aspect of our lives that you would expect we would all be quite good at it.

OLD PERCEPTIONS DIE HARD

When I first started working, many of the salespeople I encountered (and in a couple of instances, even worked with) felt to me as though they were only in the job to hit as high a sales number as they could, and earn as much bonus as they could. It must be said, this perception wasn't helped by having grown up with the regular portrayal of salespeople in TV and films as being unscrupulous, and the portrayal of the sales process as being exclusively a zero-sum game – i.e. one where someone (either the buyer or the seller) had to come off worse after having given up more than they hoped they would. And let's face it, with the salesperson being the practised expert, it was usually going to be the buyer. In short, my perception was that salespeople were all too often in it only for themselves at the expense of the next unsuspecting sucker and the profession as a whole had low moral values. In itself, there's nothing wrong with trying to learn and be the best that you can, but I find that if it comes directly at the expense of someone else, it doesn't sit well with my values. If you are a customer, it's often quite easy to spot which people are in it for themselves.

Unfortunately, sometimes the realisation can dawn too late (after you've handed over money) and while in the UK and EU there do exist laws to allow customers to claim recompense when they believe they have been mis-sold, often this can involve long and protracted efforts to pursue the matter to a satisfactory conclusion and many customers will give up purely due to this war of attrition. Furthermore, customers who have had to pursue lengthy complaints will probably not be in the mood to want to do business with that company again, something which those who focus only on the short-term consequences of their actions (getting money quickly at the expense of building long-term satisfaction to their customers) are now finding out faster than ever. A business model which seeks only to find new customers without any thought as to existing ones is not the most sustainable, as in today's ultra-connected world, news and opinion about poor customer experience spreads incredibly quickly and reputations can be made or broken overnight.

For me, one of the telling factors as to whether you might be building a sustainable sales model lies in whether your intent is congruent with the underlying reason that you are going to market, and whether that reason is pointing in the right direction. Are you genuinely trying to help your customers through delivery of your product or service?

I have been fortunate to work with some talented salespeople, and be involved in rolling out and coaching sales teams on some very well-respected sales models and methodologies. The best ones I have seen involve a combination of not just delivering sales training and adjusting internal business processes to support the sales process. They also aim to give the sales teams in question a deeper understanding of something which has an effect throughout the whole sales process, which if poorly understood can kill a sale way before any outright selling ever even has the chance to take place, but if understood well can make up for inexperience or lack of 'perfect' technique and is a constant factor in any kind of selling task – simple, complex, big or small – and that is honourable intent.

INTENT TRUMPS TECHNIQUE

Even though only a small percentage of the working population is officially involved in sales (recent estimations indicate that in the USA for example, it's about one in ten), many more of us have to sell our ideas and convince people to take certain actions and make changes every day. Practically all of us who develop and implement plans have to sell continuously to both buyers and colleagues in some way or other during our working lives. In Dan Pink's words, we are all in the business of "moving people".[41] To do this we need to be able to communicate effectively not only what action is required but also valid reasons why our audience would want to participate in it. As we have seen in earlier chapters, one of the fundamental factors influencing whether any degree of effective communication can take place is that there is trust. In initial encounters, without any other evidence, our default reaction to new things, be it people or ideas, is likely to be one of treating them as a threat.

Simply put, in new sales relationships trust does not exist in latent form, waiting to be found and used; it must be earned. Thus, I have found that the root of successful sales lies not necessarily in developing masterful negotiation techniques, or being able to keep banging the drum until my customer had been beaten into submission by pure persistence or charisma.

It lies in the very beginnings of the way in which you approach your attempts to sell. What is your intent? As with communication, can it be described as honourable or morally acceptable according to prevalent societal expectations? Your intent will more often than not dictate the manner in which you go about selling, and in turn will have a huge effect on the way in which your customer perceives you. Are you someone they can trust to deliver considered advice which is in the best mutual interests of both of you, or do they feel you are the type of person who will selfishly take what they can, but then forget about their ongoing needs the moment the ink is dry?

SUSTAINABILITY – LONG-TERM VALUE, LOW NET COST

The reason I am focusing so much on establishing solid 'moral' foundations is that this is the way to developing a long-term relationship with customers in order that they trust and enjoy their experience well enough to want to come back and do repeat business. Due to your having earned sufficient trust and credibility for them to allow you to deliver any value to them, there is less perceived risk for the customer to choose your offering again. They are familiar with it, and so their decision to choose you can be much faster and less effort-intensive than first time around. Again, we see how trust reduces the cost not only of internal processes, but also reduces the mutual cost of those you participate in with your customers.

While the factor may vary from study to study, it is estimated that the cost of acquiring a new customer can be up to 30 times the cost of maintaining relationships with an existing one. The figure I have heard most generally quoted seems to be 10 times the cost. Added to this, existing customers tend to buy more than new ones. These maxims give you a clue as to why long-term customer relationships are so valued in most industries.

Think about the chapter on change and how, thanks to our evolutionary heritage, our default reaction to it is one of apprehension because our amygdala thinks it is keeping us safe. This is where the familiarity of an existing relationship really comes into its own; unlike a new supplier, you are more of a known quantity and thus not regarded as a potential threat, so far less effort is required to demonstrate and convince an existing customer that you can be trusted to deliver both results and value in a way that is acceptable to them. If you have an existing sales relationship where your customer trusts you, don't take it for granted, but treasure and nurture it, for as we shall see shortly, from a communication opportunity standpoint alone, it puts you in the driving seat over your competitors.

Through working with (and supporting) a variety of salespeople over time who were very good at building those types of relationships where their customers would come back again and again and viewed the salesperson as a trusted advisor, I came to realise that sales isn't necessarily the root of all immorality. In fact, selling is a core part of how progress is made every day for all of us – whether we are talking about actual purchasing decisions, or decisions which just involve an individual's commitment to invest time or effort into something.

SALES IS IN FACT ALL ABOUT CHANGE MANAGEMENT

So, given its pervasiveness in our daily lives, and the impact it can have on them (and those of our customers), we can see that selling is in fact a change management process in its own right. In essence, through selling we are often attempting to establish a new way of thinking or doing things, a different choice. We may be attempting to make internal change happen through our actions or helping an external customer to do the same.

For external customers, that may mean choosing our product over a competitor's product. It may mean choosing to upgrade from the existing product or service they currently have to something that will help them realise greater net benefit. It may be choosing to buy our product or service to facilitate a new way of working or living that they haven't previously experienced – such as making the move from paper-based communication to using an electronic format, or as simple as the ease with which an electric toothbrush makes a change to our daily brushing habit. Or it may be the decision not to change things, just yet. There may be potential for change (there always is), but sometimes, if there is no burning platform, no sufficient reason for doing so, change may not be an advisable option at the present time, and we may end up helping our customer to avoid wasting time, effort and resource in trying to implement change only for change's sake, such as we saw with the techno-trap in the chapter on change.

As such, as we have seen from previous chapters, we need to start with building a 'why' for our customer, and to get the best result (understand if change is advisable and if so, elicit a strong buy-in from them to drive their desire to effect the change) we should involve them in the process from the beginning so we can fully explore and understand the situation and how we could give them value therein.

Start With A Strong Why

Given the increased number of potential variables that can affect any situation over time, it is not surprising that the further away in time something is, the more difficult we find it to predict or make firm decisions about. The closer or more familiar something is, the more comfortable we might feel making decisions about it due to there being less time for the unexpected. So, if we are trying to establish a strong 'why' to create the driving force for a project that may only come to fruition say 12 months or more into the future, it pays to establish as solid a set of credentials as possible early on that help all involved to stay focused and motivated to keep on taking the actions required.

To do this, we will need to explore our customer's situation. We may want to begin by asking them what their biggest or most important challenges or issues are with regard to the goal they are trying to achieve, and then asking them to prioritise them in descending order of importance. This can help us to focus the ensuing discussions in areas that will have the largest noticeable (and positive) impact for our customer.

So firstly you may need to ask your customer what they want – it's a pretty good place to start. But sometimes customers either don't know exactly what they want, or they think they know what they want but are, perhaps, genuinely mistaken. Please note, this is not a justification to help you feel better about trying to change their mind if they think that what you have to offer isn't right for them. Sometimes, customers simply haven't fully explored their situation, and this is probably why so many of them (in fact, so many of us, as we are all customers of some kind after all) frequently change their (our) minds part way through projects or decision processes.

Sometimes, we have to help our customers figure out whether they really do know what they want (or more to the point, need) so that they remain happy with their choice after the sale or decision is made. If we sell them a white elephant when they didn't really need one, or they regret making the decision to purchase, this will soon become apparent once the money has been exchanged and they begin to (not) use it. Relationships will deteriorate, as we push the 'blame' for the decision back on to the customer ("this is what you asked for"), when in fact what they were hoping for in contacting us was for us to use our expertise and experience to figure out if a white elephant was going to be good for them (perhaps they needed a blue one, or maybe no elephant at all; perhaps they needed a donkey instead).

So, using the right questions, we can help our customers to qualify the real needs behind their initially voiced needs. Help them find their 'why' first of all, and only then focus on the 'how'. If necessary, ask more questions to be sure both of you truly understand what it is that they need before settling on what they want. Getting it right (or closer to right) at the start is going to save you a lot of time later on.

Build A Better Customer

> *"If I'd have asked them what they wanted, they'd have said a 'faster horse'."* [42]

This quote (usually attributed to automotive industry founding father Henry Ford) reflects that 'focused only on the here and now' mindset that many customers find it hard to escape from. What I am advocating is that you get good at building a better customer. That's not a customer who is happy to just buy everything you've got, every time. I'm talking about being able to help your customer ask the right questions of their own situation so they can better understand their needs as opposed to what they think they may need at first glance.

Here's an example. For a time, I was involved in mapping business processes in my department prior to implementation of a new Enterprise Resource Planning system. In having mapped our existing processes and helping to develop how the system could provide us with information going into the future, I soon became one of the subject matter experts on our data analysis capabilities, and people would come to me for reports. During the first few weeks post-implementation, managers would ask me for a specific report giving them certain data, and without question, I would create one that gave them exactly what they had asked for. Most of the time, they would then come back and ask me to amend the report, and it was not uncommon for the same person to do so several times over.

"Could you make it look like that?"

"Is it possible to show this data too?"

"How about swapping these axes around?"

Everyone was very polite about it, but still it became tedious and frustrating for all of us, and was a very costly trial and error approach for the company. If we look at this from a supplier/customer point of view, while I effectively had a captive market (there was nowhere and no one else that my internal customers could take their business to), and I didn't have to worry about price or cash flow, my internal customers kept coming back to me over and over until I had created a solution that fitted their purpose. It was costing a lot of time to continually amend the 'product' so many times due to the fact that my customers frequently didn't know exactly what they wanted at the start of the development process.

Finally, with one manager, I stopped him at the beginning of his request and politely asked him to share with me what he was going to use it for. This alone, when put together with my experience of how people tended to use reports within the organisation, helped me to understand and marry his needs better to the capabilities of the system of which he was not aware. We soon had a host of new, highly meaningful reports that were giving our management team new insights and understanding of the business that previously they hadn't even realised were an option. It was as if I had by accident (or from another viewpoint, simply by applying my experience), stumbled on the fundamental principles of Organisational Development – working with 'clients' and objectively exploring their environments and contexts in order to provide sustainable change.[43] It took many more years before I even knew this was what I was doing. The manager was impressed at the results and speed at which he could now get useable information from the new system, and I was soon being asked if I could apply my expertise to improving our forecasting and management reporting processes – which I did successfully, gaining further credibility plus invaluable business experience and insight along the way.

From that moment on I found that before delivering anything, conducting a brief (and in some cases more in-depth) exploration of any request that came my way plus the context in which it sat made it much easier to deliver highly relevant results consistently that made my internal customers excited to work with me. Without realising it, I was taking my first steps towards following the path of consultative selling.

Explore To Establish Value

One of the cornerstones of making a buying decision is whether or not the perceived value of the choice outweighs the investment required to a sufficient degree in the mind of the buyer (whether it be in monetary, effort or other terms). The difference between the two is essentially the definition of value that the opportunity represents to the customer.

In order to provide value to a prospective customer, we must be able to demonstrate that this ratio meets or surpasses their expectations. How can you know whether or not it does? Market research and experience can give you a general feel, but the acceptable payoff can vary greatly from individual to individual and be highly dependent on their particular situation, so you must engage with your customer in order to explore it and understand better how it applies to them.

For you to provide a sales proposal or offer that is perceived by your customer as being relevant and of value to them, it must be preceded by sufficient enquiry, exploration and understanding. Only then can you find out whether or not your offering meets their expected level of value.

Preparing for Exploration

To stand a decent chance of being able to do this, you need to have open, honest, two-way dialogue between you and your customer. When the decision may have a significant impact on the customer's job, career, or life, then as we have seen from the chapter on relationships, a healthy level of trust is required for those involved to feel safe enough to share what can be sensitive information.

So we can see, to establish value through mutual exploration, there must first be trust. For existing customers, that trust may already be there – as we have seen, making it easier and faster to embark upon the exploration phase. But for new relationships, a salesperson could do a lot worse than ensuring they approach the engagement with the right mindset – that of trying to find mutual benefit. Anyone who engages a customer with purely selfish purpose will frequently be found out – it is surprising how easily and quickly our subconscious minds can recognise the patterns of tiny cues that indicate someone is not acting in our best interests. This will set off our trust alarms, leading us to close up and take either a defensive or offensive stance towards them. But if you approach your customer with the right intent – that of trying to find mutual value from your engagement – then almost without trying, your actions and words will be much more naturally congruent with your intent, putting your customer at ease and making the process much easier for you both to move through.

The mutual element of this process should also not be understated. If you have something which has an established value to your customer, then you should not shy away from reminding them if necessary that it is not to be devalued or given away for free.

The best relationships are when both parties regard one another as equal and equally deserving to benefit. A good way to recognise this symbiotic nature and maintain the correct 'balance of perceived power' is to remember that the result is going to be a combination of the marriage between what you bring to the table (your service or product plus the expertise of what is possible to achieve with it) and what the customer brings (knowledge and detail of the contextual specifics of their situation), which when used in tandem can provide an ideal fit between solution, exact need and accepted possibility.

In effect, a large part of your value will reside in whether or not you can help your potential customer to be a better customer – that is, help them to explore their situation and the potential solution options that best fit so that they can make both an informed choice and one that is highly relevant to their needs. This may include thinking beyond the here and now, and into how this solution may fit into expected future situations.

Using your experience to help your customer understand what they don't know they don't know before they commit is one of the most valuable things you can do for them, and when customers feel that degree of care being applied to their situation, trust levels rise rapidly and steeply.

For several years I had the pleasure of working with a colleague who was in sales, but also had a strong technical background. He found out that one of our organisation's major client targets in a key market for us was going to need to upgrade their IT infrastructure during the next several years, but acknowledged that they did not fully understand the new technologies they expected to have to deploy.

By providing several days' worth of obligation-free objective training on what they needed to know about the technology (purely focusing on the technical dynamics, not our offering) he indirectly positioned himself (and our company) not only as subject matter experts, but also as trusted advisors who could be relied upon to help the client understand what was important to their situation. As a result, he was invited to bid on the new project and won several millions of Euros worth of business over the next several years. The value to us of that initial investment paid off even further, as the project was highly publicised internally within the client organisation, and the project leaders promoted, giving us strong credibility and visibility into future infrastructure projects elsewhere within that client's organisation. And due to the projects leaders' new positions of influence, guess which suppliers were the first to hear about these new projects, and invited to discuss them early on with key figures involved in the decision processes?

Getting To The Real Why

Once we have a list of issues, we may wish to explore further the top two or three in order of importance. The following question can be extremely useful in this regard:

"What is it that makes this issue so important?"

This line of questioning can be pursued in several ways: the issue may be something that the customer needs to reduce or prevent from happening (a pain point that they are trying to move away from), or something that must be achieved, increased or improved (an outcome that they are trying to move towards). In each instance, it can be useful to apply a questioning methodology whose end goal is further qualification of the impact of attainment or non-attainment of the goal. This is often referred to as 'peeling the onion' – stripping away surface layers of appearance to uncover the deeper meaning that may not always be openly expressed, but which often carries a deeper level of significance.

It is for this reason that the process is also sometimes referred to as the journey of five whys – as it usually takes a maximum of asking the same question five times to get to the root reason why it is important to the individual. I have a particularly inquisitive friend who revels in calling it the 'journey of a thousand whys', (anyone with children will doubtless be well aware of this particular odyssey) but personally tend to find that in most cases, the core reason actually reveals itself after two or three iterations.

When to Beware of 'Why'

When asking why an issue is important, remember to focus on the process, not the person.

There are some situations, when you are trying to help someone find a solution to a challenge that they own, where asking why directly can make people become defensive. An example here might be if you are exploring what, if anything, has been tried before to resolve the issue and not worked. Coming straight out and asking them, "Why haven't you been able to resolve this problem so far?" can be taken as a personal affront to their capabilities. Your intent may be good (to help them explore what has already been tried in order to either figure out why it didn't work, or at least eliminate it as an option you might want to suggest as there's now no point going over old ground), but the inference behind asking the question in the following way, "Why haven't you been able to resolve this before?" tends to suggest that the lack of a solution to date is due to some kind of personal failure on their part. It is at times like this that finding another way to get the information is worth considering – finding another way to ask "Why?" One way of achieving this could be to get more specific with your line of questioning, allowing you to phrase it more objectively, and remembering to focus on what has happened in the process, so for example you might ask:

"What other efforts have been tried to solve this problem?"

See how this removes much, if not all of the personal aspect? Use of the passive voice means we are no longer suggesting that the failure or absence of previous attempts to solve the problem are directly the fault of the person you are speaking to, but instead simply enquires if there have been previous attempts or activities and, if so, you can then go on to explore what prevented them from succeeding. It places the focus on fixing the process, not the person.

The fact that you're here discussing with your customer other ways to resolve the issue is enough to tell everyone that they didn't fully work, so there's no need to underline this fact, but by depersonalising the focus, you have then succeeded in asking the exploratory question in a more objective and acceptable way. If needed, you could explore the results further by asking, "And how did they work out?"

The key thing to recognise here is that you have avoided creating a potential threat to your customer's personal status (the suggestion that they are not up to performing their job), and have thereby reduced the chances that they will react defensively and close down communications with you. This would be a natural and entirely expected reaction, but is the last thing you want if you are to conduct a genuinely candid, mutual exploration of the subject, which is vital to making progress in understanding it.

Similarly, in peeling the onion, if you feel that asking directly why they believe something has to happen or must be changed makes your customer too uncomfortable, you can soften your approach by using the passive voice,

"So if this was achieved, what would that mean?"

"And what would achieving this enable to happen?"

Alternatively, you could try exploring variants on the consequences of being unable to achieve the change, for example:

"What would happen if this wasn't achieved?"

In each instance, we are depersonalising the exploration and focusing on the process not the person, removing possible triggers that might cause our customer to hide from or deflect attention from the real issues or impacts so that they feel comfortable and safe enough exploring to the point where we can find a reason that we are able to quantify.

Quantify, Quantify, Quantify

Why do we want to quantify it? Because hard data is easy for our minds (and the minds of others who need to 'get on board' with the project) to remember and understand in terms of its relativity and importance to other things that we might be tempted to spend our time or resources on. Unlike abstract descriptions which can have a massively wide range of meaning from individual to individual, quantified data is more clear, concise and helps to justify decisions on the project more easily when it may come up against obstacles that need to be overcome, or challenges as to its merit (such as whether there is even a need for it). If it can be measured, it can be managed, and because of its simple brevity, quantified data is frequently also easy for customers to remember.

When quantifying, it is useful to provide some measurement parameters in order for everyone to get a clear idea of the scale and impact of the challenge:

- How are you currently measuring or quantifying this?
- What is the current score or value of where things are now?
- At what level do you intend this score or value to be once change has been implemented?
- So what is the difference between current and target scores?
- And over what period of time should this be realised?

This will deliver some hard data to support justification to the customer and for them to use within their organisation to garner resource and support as to why this is important and must be acted upon now. In effect, you have helped them to build a business case – conforming to Steve's Golden Rule Of Working Here number 1: helping the people we want to make a decision to be able to justify it to their boss, and easy for their boss to justify it to their boss, and so on, and so on.

They may already have the answers to this ready (a well-prepared customer), but if they do not, you have already begun to generate value for them by helping them to make their decision-making process more efficient. If it is impossible for them to quantify the impact, then you may at least be able to get them to qualify it – and may ask them to score the importance to the organisation of reaching the goal or preventing the problem. Scoring is a relative concept, so depending on your customer, you may want to assign them a defined scale to utilise – e.g. ask them to rate importance and impact, with 1 being "It wouldn't matter at all if we didn't achieve this" to 5 "We could not continue to operate if we did not achieve this goal." Often you find that this exercise can open new lines of questioning and exploration (e.g. "Why would that be the case?") that can later reveal a quantifiable impact.

So, in defining the impact of achieving or not achieving resolution to a specific issue, we can begin to understand in our customer's own words what value might look like to them, and whether or not the return on investment that we have to offer is likely to be perceived as of sufficient value. This is vital if we want our customers to work with us, especially if we want them to consider anything other than simply price. If this happens, it suggests that your customer doesn't believe there to be any other difference in value between you and the alternative options. So, in getting to this stage you can give yourself a pat on the back as you've just created a 'why' which is strong because:

- It's relevant.

- It's defined by the customer in their own terms – and so is likely to be a lot more credible, acceptable and memorable.

- It's hard (quantified) – so will be a lot easier for everyone to see, understand and use.

- Your credibility will be higher as you have already delivered them value (for free) by helping them to see what needed to be seen before anything has been set in motion.

Assuming that there was value to reveal, now that you both have a strong reason as to why the project should go ahead, plus the expected return that would be necessary to agree to continue seeking a resolution, you are able to explore more of the details around how it can possibly go ahead. These can include details on what limits or restraints exist in terms of time available, quality/specification levels required, and resource and money available. This is also the time when you may get a feeling for how much a solution is going to cost, plus how much your customer is willing to pay in order to achieve the identified results that achieving the resolution to their issues would bring. And if they marry up (hopefully you already did some basic research to increase the chances of a match here before even contacting a customer; there's no point trying to sell a multi-million pound car fleet contract to a one-man band), you are now in a position to propose a highly relevant solution that will provide demonstrable return on the most important challenges that your customer is facing.

Never Ignore The Elephant

One more simple yet powerful principle that when applied may not always appear to deliver a lot of short-term gain, but can save you a lot of time and reap significant returns long into the future. If you genuinely have the best interests of your customer at heart, then you will also be prepared to halt progress if you come up against an obstacle that looks like it could derail the progress you are both hoping to make. If you see any indicator that given the context your envisaged solution simply cannot work, do not shy away from it, hoping that it will magically disappear. The prospect of losing a potential customer may scare you, but clarifying whether or not it is an unsurmountable problem is preferable to wasting both of your time.

Being honest and brave enough to raise potential problems you see will benefit both you and your customer, as it will allow you to explore them and figure out if they really are genuine show-stoppers (in which case your customer will appreciate your integrity) or if the application of other effort or ideas can enable you to move past them. If you've done your initial exploration well, you may find that your customer is extremely committed to help you find a way past them, as they want the results that you have both envisioned could be attained.

If you have to withdraw from a selling relationship, I would recommend that at all times you try your best to do so graciously without apportioning blame. An objective and polite acknowledgement that it would be in neither of your best interests to proceed can help protect bridges, relationships and trust that may have been built to date and which may come in handy at some point in the future. After all, with the super-connected continuously changing world we now live in, who knows what new opportunities may come your way, from where they may emanate, and upon whom you may depend for support, help or recommendation?

Don't Forget To Deliver!

Of course, it should go without saying but as in each of these examples I have cited, delivering on your promises and continued service expectations post-sale is of equal importance to sustainable selling relationships as the initial establishment of trust and credibility. As the saying goes, trust can take years to build and mere seconds to destroy. Once again, in the long-term relationship stakes, intent is king. While most people can accept that mistakes are made, most are more ready to accept them and move on if they see proactive attempts on the part of the supplier to try and remedy the situation or reduce the impact on the customer.

Remember Your Internal Customers

It is perhaps worth recognising that the customers we are probably more likely to envisage when talking about sales are external customers. But a largely forgotten group is the internal customer – people within our organisation with whom we may work directly and need to ask to participate in group processes, or contribute their expertise or effort at some point to activities in which we are involved.

Understanding that your internal customers have similar needs and react in similar ways to your external ones can go a long way towards making you the sort of person that others respect, trust and want to work with (doesn't this sound familiar?).

If you don't understand their needs in a given circumstance, they will be less likely to want to work with you in the future. If you show little regard for their requirements (as part of the overall process in which you are both involved) then you may be viewed simply as a 'taker' – someone who imposes for their own benefit, regardless of the effect it may have upon others, and your working relationship with them may become strained and uncomfortable.

The effect of providing poor service to internal customers will similarly result in higher costs (in terms of effort at least) to fix or resolve problems, loss of credibility, and ultimately even your job if the organisation decides it needs to evaluate its structure and staffing levels.

But even if at the very least you can provide them with a suitable 'why' (why it is important that the business achieves a particular objective) and work with them to understand how you can make it easier for them to perform their role in the process, then your effort and intent will be rewarded.

Being held in high regard by your internal customers can have an extremely beneficial effect on your career, as organisations and managers who recognise the value of staff with this type of attitude will go a long way to ensuring you are happy in your work and have good reasons to want to stay, whether they be in the form of financial recompense, opportunities to learn, career progression opportunities or other perks.

What's Inside Will Come Out

In fact the satisfaction of internal customers is viewed in quality circles as being a precursor to the satisfaction of external customers. If the organisation is operating with a philosophy of ensuring that its own processes and attitudes are geared towards delivering effective and efficient experiences at the micro-process level, then the externally delivered results are highly likely to be the product of these many individual internal commitments to excellence, much like the many marginal gains that propelled Team GB to so many cycling titles. As a species, being (generally) happiest and most effective when in groups and working together requires constant effort to help keep the group together and help individuals within it to take actions which are of mutual community benefit.[44] This in itself requires constant selling: sometimes subtle ('who fancies going to the burger joint for lunch?'); sometimes more overt ('we're going to need a willing volunteer'). In observing the communication dynamics of both groups and between individual successful salespeople and their customers, we can begin to see these common factors which make them work, at play.

And, in light of the view that we are constantly selling, then wouldn't it stand to reason that by learning some of the more effective (and dare I say it, more reputable) methods employed by successful sales people, we could improve mutual cooperation and go a long way towards improving our progress in our everyday working lives and beyond? If you have made the decision to beef up your skills and turn yourself into a lean, mean selling machine who is able to effect buy-in to change with seemingly effortless elegance, then please for the sake of us all, the generations of the future, and for your own sustained success, make sure you have the right intent! As Dan Pink sums up in *To Sell Is Human*, to be sure you are being of service in every selling opportunity you face, ask yourself firstly whether or not a purchase will improve the life of the person buying (sometimes this may need to be in terms of the bigger picture or longer term view), and secondly, will the world be a better place once this has happened. "If the answer to either of these is no, you're doing something wrong."[45]

SUMMARY

- The sales process has been stigmatised by decades of misplaced intent and continual media portrayal of it.

- Openness and honesty are required to mutually explore if and how you might be able to help your customer. Trust is required for this to be possible.

- Starting with the right intent will go a long way to building trust and can even guide your technique.

- Building long-term sustainable relationships is far more cost-effective than chasing new ones.

- Sales is in fact a form of change management – customers need to be involved in establishing a strong 'why' and finding solutions that might answer their challenges.

- Peeling the onion to help customers understand their actual needs adds value before you have sold anything.

- Quantifying current challenges and expected results can make the value a solution could deliver much more tangible.

- Asking why is great, but beware of making your customer feel inadequate about their ability to resolve issues on their own – try focusing on the process, not the person.

- Slow down to clarify if obstacles are genuine show-stoppers or not – you may save everyone a lot of time, effort and cost.

- Go the extra mile to ensure you deliver on your promises.

- Treat your internal customers as if they were external ones – they require your respect and support in order to do their job.

ACKNOWLEDGEMENTS

In terms of preparing me to make it this far, I would like to thank my late grandad Archie Anderton for relentlessly and joyfully feeding my young thirst for knowledge; my grandmothers Joyce and Eileen for reminding me that every moment of life has the potential for laughter; my grandad Roland for showing me what humility is; my father for helping me see how important it can be to develop a strong sense of objectivity; my mother for providing me with an incredibly safe, loving and happy home, and my sister for showing me just how resilient the human spirit is.

For the book specifically, huge thanks must go to my wife Inna, for allowing me the time to focus on it to such a great degree and to my kids for just being themselves. You are the twinkling stars of the future and provide me with both incredible fun and reminders of what the important things in life are.

I would also like to thank many of the people that I have worked with over the years and some with whom I will never get the chance to work with again. It is from you that I drew inspiration for the need for such a book, many of the lessons within it, and the encouragement to actually write it. You know who you are, and I hope some of you can take a little pride and satisfaction that you have all, in your own ways, contributed to its fruition.

ABOUT THE AUTHOR

Steve Chad is a marketing professional, parent and author. Post-grad studies in Organisational Development and an accumulation of observations from over 20 years working with small, medium and global companies inspired him to publish *The Tao Of Work Fu*. When not contemplating retirement from international sport, he can be found pursuing enrichment of the soul through the finding and sharing of meaning. Oh, and he absolutely loves to help! You can meet him at http://taoofworkfu.com.

NOTES

(Endnotes)

1. Bruce Thomas, *Bruce Lee: Fighting Spirit: A Biography*, 1994

2. Mihaly Csikszentmihalyi, *Good Business: Leadership, Flow and the Making of Meaning*, 2004

3. Robert Burns, *Tae a Moose*, 1785

4. Edward N. Lorenz, '*Predictability; Does the Flap of a Butterfly's wings in Brazil set off a Tornado in Texas?*' AAAS 139th Meeting, 1972

5. Dr. Steve Peters, *The Chimp Paradox*, 2012

6. David Rock, *Your Brain At Work*, 2009

7. Elizabeth Kübler-Ross, *On Death and Dying*, 1969

8. Laurence Cruz, '*Chief Disruption Officer: The New Role*', *The network Cisco's Technology News Site*, May 2015. *Used with the permission of http://thenetwork.cisco.com/.*

9. Malcolm Gladwell, *Outliers: The Story of Success*, 2009

10. Josh Kaufman, *The First 20 Hours: How To Learn Anything…Fast*, 2013

11. John P. Kotter, *Leading Change*, 1996

12. *http://www.joelbarker.com*

13. robertr, '*20 Tips On Overcoming Fear*' *blog.dalecarnegie.com*, 5th June 2009

14. Jonathan Haidt, *The Happiness Hypothesis*, 2006

15. *Star Wars Episode IV: A New Hope*, (film) 1977

16. *http://www.intel.co.uk/content/www/uk/en/history/museum-gordon-moore-law.html*

17. *Road House*, (film) 1989

18. *http://www.goodreads.com/author/quotes/570218.Dalai_Lama_XIV*

19. Stephen M. R. Covey, *The Speed of Trust: The One Thing That Changes Everything*, 2008

20. Barry Schwartz, *The Paradox of Choice: Why More Is Less*, 2005

21. *http://www.notable-quotes.com/e/edison_thomas.html*

22. *http://www.bbc.co.uk/sport/0/olympics/19174302*

23. http://www.theguardian.com/sport/2004/feb/22/rugbyunion.deniscampbell

24. Mihaly Csikszentmihalyi, *Flow: The Psychology of Happiness*, 1990

25. Robert Kelsey, *What's Stopping You?: Why Smart People Don't Always Reach Their Potential and How You Can*, 2011

26. *http://www.goodreads.com/author/quotes/657773.Jim_Rohn*

27. Daniel H. Pink, *A Whole New Mind: Why Right-Brainers Will Rule The Future*, 2008

28. *https://prelectur.stanford.edu/lecturers/hofstadter/analogy.html*

29. Stephen R. Covey, *The 7 Habits of Highly Effective People: Powerful Lessons in Personal Change (25th Anniversary Edition)*, 2013

30. David Rock, *Your Brain At Work*, 2009

31. John Teasdale, leading researcher at Oxford and Cambridge Universities and pioneer of Mindfulness-based Cognitive Therapy

32. Felice Leonardo Buscaglia, Author, Speaker & Professor in the Department of Special Education, University of Southern California

33. *http://news.bbc.co.uk/1/hi/3254852.stm*

34. Matthew Sayed, *Bounce: The Myth of Talent and the Power of Practice*, 2011

35. Douglas Hofstadter, *I Am A Strange Loop*, 2008

36. Josh Kaufman, *The First 20 Hours: How To Learn Anything...Fast*, 2013

37. *http://epltt.coe.uga.edu/index.php?title=Bloom's_Taxonomy*

38. Matthew Sayed, *Bounce: The Myth of Talent and the Power of Practice*, 2011

39. *http://donaldclarkplanb.blogspot.co.uk/2012/04/ebbinghaus-1850-1909-memory-genius.html*

40. *https://prelectur.stanford.edu/lecturers/hofstadter/analogy.html*

41. Daniel H. Pink, *To Sell Is Human*, 2012

42. *http://quoteinvestigator.com/2011/07/28/ford-faster-horse/*. Apparently there is little evidence to substantiate that Ford ever said it, but it still fulfils its point, demonstrating that merely extending progress further in the same direction is not always the answer. Sometimes a burst of lateral insight is required, and for that, the distance and objectivity of an external observer can help.

43. Edgar Schein, *Process Consultation: Its Role In Organisational Development*, 1969

44. Richard Dawkins, *The God Delusion*, 2006

45. Daniel H. Pink, *To Sell Is Human*, 2012

Printed in Great Britain
by Amazon